MW00975873

With Greater Power

*The Secret To a
Spirit-Powered Life*

Robert M. Tenery
J. Steve Sells

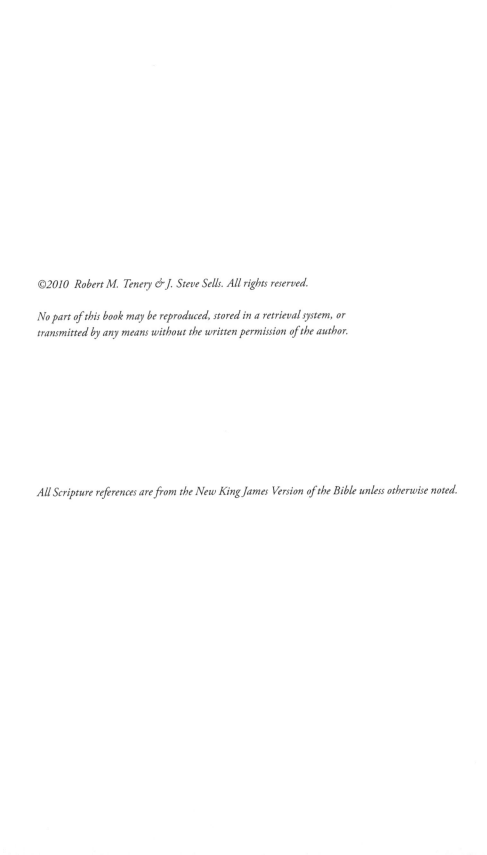

©2010 Robert M. Tenery & J. Steve Sells. All rights reserved.

No part of this book may be reproduced, stored in a retrieval system, or transmitted by any means without the written permission of the author.

All Scripture references are from the New King James Version of the Bible unless otherwise noted.

Dedication

We dedicate this book to our wives, Shirley Sells and Willo'deane Tenery who have labored with us, prayed for us and encouraged us through many years of pastoral ministry.

Acknowledgment

We acknowledge the untiring efforts of Willo'deane Tenery in the preparation of this manuscript. Her assistance and suggestions have been invaluable in the production of this book.

Foreword

Terror Alert!

It has become an accepted part of the warp and woof of our lives in North America. We trudge through airports as they announce over the loud speakers that the threat level is *Yellow, Orange* (or <u>whatever appropriate color</u>). Those of us, who have heard it regularly, sadly enough, let it go in one ear and out the other.

Perhaps, one of the most discussed threats among the experts is the threat to the United States **Power Grid**. Divided into three major sections, it is responsible for supplying all the electrical power to America daily - it is the key to running almost everything we take for granted. If terrorists were to take out a part of the grid, it could shut down the electronic pulse system that would paralyze one or more major cities in an instant. Wall Street, with its' massive integrated computer tracking system, would be helpless. The booking of flights and the air traffic control system along with Google, Yahoo, Facebook and Twitter would all be out!! Electric pumps, water systems and sewage treatment plants as well as incinerators would all be down. The country would be in total chaos!

The scary thing is that we have had a foretaste of just how scary it could be. The massive power surge in the summer of 2003 that began at a power plant in Ohio tripped a "cascading failure" which resulted in a complete blackout of New York City, much of the East Coast, and even a part of the Midwest. **Forty-five million people** were literally "in the dark" and losses in the tens of billions of dollars exploded onto the scene.

However, isn't there a danger just as great, if not greater, to Christ's church today? Despite pockets of good things and effective ministry there seems to be an absence of **power**. In a day when there are more Christian CDs, conferences, books, activities, dollars, and trips than ever before, the culture of America continues to move further and further from its Judeo-Christian roots and the church seems to have less and less impact. Why?

Could it be that the "power grid" of the church—the **Holy Spirit** and **His power**—has been disrupted and we don't even recognize it? My friends, Bob Tenery and Steve Sells, have addressed just that question. We have bigger and costlier buildings, but too often less and less power. We generate big crowds, but too often experience little **lasting impact**. We are drowning in **information**, but too often bereft of **transformation**.

Bob and Steve call us back to the **basics**. While it may not be easy… it is simple. Only the power of Christ, **in and through His people**, can accomplish the plans God has for His world…and for you! With biblical mastery, historical accuracy and practical application the writers call us away from a "feel good" religion to a **dynamic, transformational faith**. They are not stuck in theory; they show us how to live it out in everyday practicality.

So, if you feel like you are in need of a fresh measure of God's power, this book is for you. Or, if you feel you've been experiencing a lot of motion without meaning in your faith walk, this book is for you! If you just need a fresh perspective that gets away from "easy believeism" and moves you to a **dynamic life change**, this book is for you.

I found this book to be a wonderful friend as I sat by the fire, grabbed a cup of coffee and did a gut check of getting back to the basics of where the **power** comes from in my journey of faith. Why don't you grab some coffee, or hot tea? Maybe pick up a soft drink or an iced latte. Get quiet. Open your heart, and pray this prayer "… Search me O God, and know my heart; try me and know my thoughts…" (Psalm 139: 23) and expect God to do something special—restore the **power** in your journey.

Dr. Robert E, Reccord
President, Total Life Impact Ministries
Executive Director, Counsel for National Policy,
Washington, DC

Contents

This book is written for the use of denominational leaders, pastors, staff workers and lay leaders in the local Church.   It may be used in a sermon series, Wednesday night Bible studies, weekday Bible studies, home Bible studies or older youth groups. There are **Points for Discussion** at the end of each section to aid those who teach the book. The book may also be used for the edification of the average Christian in the pew. Particular care has been taken to make the book readable and usable for the laity.

Introduction

Critical are these days in which the church must minister. A time when there was more hostility toward Christians and their church is beyond the memory of most Christians who are alive today. We are receiving reports that atheistic clubs are being formed on many college campuses and some high schools. Signs are appearing on some city buses with an atheistic message. The church is being attacked both from without and within. It is not a climate in which a casual church can survive.

The church that can minister in this kind of world must be a Spirit powered church. Every functioning entity must have a source of power. The source of power may be electrical, diesel, gas or coal. Other sources of power would include wind, solar or battery. The source may even be nuclear. However, the power must be adequate. It is impossible to power a huge truck with a lawn mower engine. Likewise, the church is the body of Christ (Ephesians 2: 22-23). Thus, it is a functioning organism. It must be **powered** in order to function. It cannot be powered by human intellect, aesthetic worship services, beautiful and comfortable facilities or even unusual and attractive architecture. These things may be good, but the church can function as the Lord intended only if it is **powered** by the **Holy Spirit.** After His resurrection Jesus declared to his followers that *"all power ...."* had been given to Him in Heaven and in Earth. The "therefore" of that commission was that they should go and teach all nations on the basis of the **power** that had been given unto Him and that He would be with them even unto the end of the world (Matthew 28:18). His specific charge to them was: *"... tarry in the city of Jerusalem until you are endued with power from on high."* (Luke 24:49) In His final charge to them He told them that they would *"... be baptized with the **Holy Spirit** not many days from now"* (Acts 1:5) and that they would *"... receive power when the **Holy Spirit** has come upon you."* (Acts 1:8a) As a result, they would become witnesses of Jesus *"in Jerusalem, and in all Judea and Samaria, and to the end of the earth."* (Acts 1:8b) Jesus final commission to His followers made it clear that the **Holy Spirit** would be the source of **power** for the **New Testament church**. It **is** only the **Spirit** powered church that can successfully confront a secular and skeptical world.

We were appalled when the historian, Eugene Genovese, an atheist and Marxist, stated, "When I read much protestant theology and religious history today, I have the warm feeling that I am in the company of fellow non-believers." The shock was compounded when the same report stated that Gerd Ludeman, a world-renowned theologian, declared that, "I no longer describe myself as a Christian." He is a professor of New Testament and director of the Institute of Early Christian Studies at Gottingen University in Germany. He is also the author of the influential book Heretics (1995). His position was that heretics have been right all the time, and that the church has conjured a supernatural Jesus to further its own cause. Concerning the death and burial of Jesus, Ludeman said, "So, let us say quite specifically: the tomb of Jesus was not empty but full and his body did not disappear but rotted away." Ludeman criticized liberal theologians and said that many church officials no longer believe in their creeds but they simply "interpret" the words into meaninglessness. He contends that they simply try to reformulate Christian doctrine into something that they can believe and still claim to be Christians. He describes liberal theology as "contemptible." He further shocked the world by saying: "I don't think that Christians know what they mean when they proclaim Jesus as spirit lord of the world. That is a massive claim. If you took that seriously, you would probably have to be a fundamentalist. If you can't be a fundamentalist, then you should give up Christianity for the sake of honesty." This, however, is not the end of disturbing developments.

The Shocking Headline

The headline read, "Most American Christians do not believe that **Satan** or the **Holy Spirit** exists." It was hard to believe! How could this be? As we read further into the report, we were saddened to read that more than one-fifth of American Christians believe that Jesus sinned while He lived on earth, with another seven percent agreeing "somewhat" with that statement, and only forty-six percent strongly disagreed with that idea. Forty-nine percent of those surveyed agreed that the Holy Spirit is only a symbol, but not a living entity; and they believe that the Bible is not completely accurate in all of the principles that are taught within its pages. Thirty-three percent of the self-defined Christians in America agree that the Bible, Koran and Book of Mormon all teach the same truths simultaneously. It seemed almost unbelievable but it came from the **Barna Group,** which is a well-known and highly respected survey group that has been found to be fair and kind toward American Christians.

What is to be the church's response to a people who do not believe in Satan or the Holy Spirit? As the church confronts these shocking developments in our society, it does no good to pretend that there is no such force in the world as evil; and that there is no such being as Satan. **Jesus certainly did not!** When Jesus was baptized, the **Holy Spi**rit descended upon Him in the bodily form of a Dove (Luke 3: 21-22) Soon after his baptism, Jesus was *"led by the Spirit into the wilderness."* (Luke 4: 1) The descending of the Holy Spirit upon Jesus at his baptism was like a keystone of His ministry. Now, He was about to begin His Galilean ministry at about thirty years of age. He had *"increased in **wisdom** and **stature** and in **favor** with **God** and **man**."* (Luke 2: 52) Now the God/Man - the Messiah- had received a special infilling of the Spirit and the first thing He was led to do was to deal with Satan in the wilderness. Each time Satan tempted Him, Jesus responded with **Scripture**. What a lesson for us! At the end of the period of temptation, angels came and ministered to Him (Matthew 4: 11). Now, Jesus was ready for His ministry. When He *"returned in the **power** of the **Spirit** to Galilee, news of Him went out through all the surrounding region."* (Luke 4: 14) Moreover, Jesus was very sensitive to satanic activity. He rebuked Peter when Peter took Him aside to rebuke Him after Jesus stated his messianic mission. Jesus made it clear to Peter that he had allowed Satan to enter into him, and that he was offensive to the Lord when Satan was controlling his life (Matthew 16:23). It was in Luke 22:31 that Jesus warned Peter that Satan would sift him as wheat, but Jesus assured him of His prayers for him.

When James and John asked Jesus about calling down fire upon a Samaritan village because they were not hospitable to them, Jesus gave them a rebuke when He said, *"You do not know what manner of **Spirit** you are of."* (Luke 9: 55) In Mark 5: 1-19 we read of Jesus' dealings with the Gadarene demoniac who gave his name as "Legion" because many devils had entered into him. Of course, Peter learned his lesson well. In his letter, he warns his readers to be sober and vigilant because *"Your **adversary** the devil walks about like a roaring lion seeking whom he may devour."* Peter's admonition is that we should, *"Resist him, steadfast in the faith, knowing that the same sufferings are experienced by your brotherhood in the world."* (I Peter 5: 8-9)

How could anyone doubt that there is a real personal Satan in the world? What would cause a woman to kill her own baby and hide it away in the trunk of her car? Who, but Satan, could cause a Cleveland man to rape and kill eleven women, leaving their bodies to putrefy and decay in and around his house. Our nation mourned with Amish families on October second of 2005 after a milk truck driver (Charlie Roberts) entered an Amish school and began shooting students, leaving five girls dead. A psychologist from John Hopkins University said: "He could not deal with the **demons within.**" The psychologist was **right.** What pastor has not had to deal with people who are under satanic influence? This is not to suggest that we should ever take a "Flip Wilson" ("The devil made me do it.") approach to the personal devil. However, it does suggest that we must take satanic influences seriously. We must deal with Satan forthrightly as Jesus did. It will be impossible for Christians to resist his temptations if they refuse to recognize his influence in their daily lives. Prayer and Bible study should be a daily reminder of the power of God to help overcome these temptations. It can be disastrous to take Satan lightly without engaging the power of the **Holy Spirit** to deal with him.

At one point in my ministry, I served as a correctional chaplain in a facility at which I had to deal with Satan worshippers. We were able to reach some of them but not all. The big holiday of Satan worshippers is "All Hallows Eve" (Halloween). Usually, on that date I was up most of the night trying to deal with their antics. They would slash their wrists and attempt to draw a satanic altar on the floor of their cells with their own blood. We had to keep anything away from them that they could use to hurt themselves or others. The reader will understand my dismay when I see Christians decorating their houses and lawns at Halloween more than they do to celebrate Christmas or Easter. The satanic calendar calls for celebrating "All Hallows Eve" by the raping of a virgin. Yet, Christians are sometimes shocked to see their young people so acceptant of Satanism. Christians and sometimes churches lend credibility to this pagan holiday through their activities!

Facing a Daunting Task

It is in the midst of this atmosphere, when the world is careening toward chaos, that church leaders are wondering why their churches are plateauing or declining. Clinicians and theoreticians are exerting their mental, emotional and physical energies in an attempt to ameliorate the churches' maladies. Ecclesiastical thinkers have offered various prescriptions that they believe will heal the church. They have tried everything from contemporary music to casual dress; personal enrichment seminars; support groups and various other activities. However, those activities, while they may do some good, have failed to produce the revitalized congregations for which pastors and other leaders have hoped and prayed. A pall of discouragement has fallen across the ministries of many pastors. A megachurch pastor recently said to me: "My people are a mile wide and an inch deep." At a recent pastor's conference, a long time senior pastor asked this writer: "What is wrong? What can we do?"

Our Purpose

It is the purpose of this book to help equip pastors and lay people in the churches to minister with power and effectiveness in this kind of world. This is not the first time that the church has been forced to minister in a hostile world. Peter and John were cast into prison because they preached, through Jesus, the resurrection from the dead on Solomon's porch (Acts 4:2). When Peter was hauled before the high priests, he successfully dealt with them. How? We find the answer in Acts 4: 8; when Peter, *filled with the **Holy Spirit**,*" answered them. When the early church faced a hostile world, the thing that made the difference was the **Holy Spirit** and that is what will make the difference today.

Yes, almost without exception, Hollywood portrays Christians as being ignorant, unlearned, flat earth people who handle snakes. These portrayals take place in the face of the fact that some of the greatest colleges and universities of this nation were founded by Christians. The question that should be honestly asked is, "How many have the atheists founded?" The answer is obvious. Yes, we serve in a hostile world populated by many who are willing to wave a jaunt farewell to God and declare that any further trek with Him will be on their own terms. They feel that they have come of age, all in the frame of the information "super highway." Their IPods, Blackberries and digital flat screens have told them so. Many Christian leaders are willing to stand by with a wistful air as though they are pallbearers at the world's funeral.

Yes, many Christians are suffering for their faith even in our homeland. A principal and a coach at the Pace High School in Florida faced possible prison sentences and loss of all their retirement benefits because they prayed over their meal. They were charged with "criminal contempt". Christians

5

were dismayed when a Federal Judge in Galveston, Texas ordered that prayers could not be offered at graduation exercises. He said, "Make no mistake; the court is going to have a United States Marshall in attendance at the graduation. If any student offends the court, that student will be summarily arrested and face up to six months incarceration in the Galveston County jail for contempt of court." He further threatened, "Anyone who violates this order, no kidding, is going to wish that he or she had died as a child when this court gets through with him." (Reported by Janet Porter, WorldNet Daily November 8, 2009) However, we must not be discouraged. One young woman went into his court and challenged his ruling and she won. The Texas legislature has now passed a law ensuring protection of religious freedom.

Nevertheless, there are those faithful Christians who have stood by the Word of God and the Church of our Lord who are discouraged. What are we to say to them? We can and must say, *"Be faithful weary pilgrim, the gate that is straight and the way that is narrow is still open. Christ is still alive. God is still sovereign and the Holy Spirit of God is real. Yes! A thousand times, Yes! There is a balm in Gilead to heal the sin sick soul."* (Jeremiah 8:22) It is those people, **empowered** by the **Holy Spirit,** who can confront a wicked world and make a diff erence. Th ey are the hope of the church.

The Church, by God's design, must be **Holy Spirit** powered in order to succeed in doing the will of God. The Spirit must accompany purpose. Without the power of the Spirit, purpose only becomes wishful thinking. The Holy Spirit gives power to the paper and ink of Holy Scripture. The Holy Spirit guides us in the proper understanding of the Scripture. Without the Holy Spirit, we cannot even understand the deep truths of the Word of God. The Spirit is our comforter and our guide, our Paraclete (παρακλητος)!

Irenaeus once said, "Where the church is, there is also the Spirit of God; and where the spirit of God is, there is also the church." It is the Holy Spirit that guards the church against the gates of Hell (Matthew 16: 18). It was John Stott who said, "We do not need to wait for the Holy Spirit to come; he came on the day of Pentecost. He has never left the church." We have all of **Him**. Does He have all of **us**!

Present day Christians and their churches must learn from and draw strength from early church stalwarts, such as Peter and John, who bore witness in a world that was unbelievably hostile. When the council saw their boldness and they "… *perceived that they were uneducated and untrained men, they marveled. And they realized that they had been with Jesus."* (Acts

4:13) Following Jesus is what made the diff erence in Jerusalem. A hostile world is no match for the power of the **Holy Spirit.**

Dear reader, we ask that you read this book carefully and prayerfully. It is the desire of the authors that this book be used of the Holy Spirit to bring to you a holy boldness that will empower you in your life and make of you a channel of the **Holy Spirit** that not only empowers you but the congregation of which you are a part. If this happens, this book will fulfill the hearts' desire of its authors. We believe that a relationship with the Holy Spirit, the third person of the Trinity, is a foundational belief of Christianity. Much of our ministry may be to those discouraged and doubting fellow church members. The idea some Christians have that Jesus was not sinless, as was referred to earlier, is not only a denial of Hebrews 4:15, but it is a denial of the teachings of Jesus, Himself (John 8:46-47). We are thoroughly convinced that when churches utilize the **power** and **ministry** of the **Holy Spirit**, they will not embrace such heresies but will regain their footing as representatives of Christ on earth. We affirm and embrace without hesitation or mental reservation the declaration of Jesus in John 16 that the Holy Spirit is now administering the affairs of the Kingdom of God. That is the basic theme and thrust of this book. We pray that every reader of this work will not only read it prayerfully but will be searching the Scriptures daily (Acts 17:11), that you may become that channel of blessing and power in your church.

Step One
Understand Who He Is

The Holy Spirit is more than a dove in a stained glass window. That is a beautiful and touching symbol of the Holy Spirit but it is not the essence of the Holy Spirit. The Spirit powered church must get beyond the symbols to the essence. The Holy Spirit is not simply a power or an influence. While He is powerful and does have great influence, He is more than that. It is essential for a church to understand that the Holy Spirit is a **person**. The Scripture always refers to the Holy Spirit in the masculine gender. He is not only a person but He is the third person of the **Trinity**. He is a part of the Godhead who was active in creation.

The people of God need never be dissuaded concerning the **Trinity**. We are Trinitarians. The Trinity is well established in the very first line of the first book of the Bible. In Genesis 1:1 the Scripture reads, *"In the beginning God created the heavens and the earth."* The word for God (Elohim) is a plural noun. This is followed by a singular verb (Bara). This structure clearly establishes the fact of a triune God. Moreover, creation activity included the Holy Spirit as well as the Lord Jesus, the Son of God. It was the **"Spirit"** that moved upon the face of the waters. John reminded us that Jesus was active in creation. He said, *"All things were made through Him, and without Him nothing was made that was made."* (John 1: 3) In Genesis 1: 26 we have the account of the creation of man. The message is clear: *"Then God said, 'Let **Us** make man in **Our** image, according to **Our** likeness; ..."* The plural pronoun **"us"** is in perfect harmony with the plural noun for God (Elohim) which underscores the **Trinity.** Because man is a **spiritual** being, he, unlike the animal kingdom, has the unique ability, including intellectual, emotional and volitional abilities, to have **fellowship** with God. It is, therefore, clear that God the Father, God the Son and God the Holy Spirit were all active as **one** in the creation of the universe. The Roman letter tells us that the Holy Spirit has a mind and therefore can think (Romans 8:27 NKJV). There can never be any doubt that, *"Now He who searches the hearts knows what the **mind** of the **Spirit** is." Having* a mind means that He also has knowledge. Paul declares to the Corinthians that *"For what man knows the things of a man except the* ***spirit*** *of the man which is in him? Even so no one knows the things of God except the* ***Spirit*** *of God."* (I Corinthians 2:11)

Active in The Old Testament

The Spirit was active in the Old Testament. The word in the Old Testament that is translated "Spirit" (ruach) means breath, wind or spirit. Therefore, when God formed man of the dust of the ground, He *"breathed into his nostrils the breath of life; and man became a* ***living soul."*** This is not said of any animal creature but only of man and this is the thing that sets man apart. Man is not just a higher form of animal life. Man is a **living soul**. It is the work of the Spirit that makes him a living soul.

The fact that the Spirit was active in the creation of the universe and active in man's becoming a living soul tells us that the Spirit has great power. We must always remember that the Holy Spirit is not apart from God but His power is distinctive and represents a distinct **function** of the Godhead. We see then, that the Holy Spirit represents the **outgoing energy of God** in the universe and in the life of man.

The presence of the Holy Spirit is also synonymous with the presence of God (Psalm 139:7). We find the same theme in Isaiah when the prophet is rebuking the people of Israel for their dependence upon Egypt as their protector. Isaiah reminds the people of Judah that the Egyptians are *"men and not God and their horses flesh, and not* ***spirit***.*" (*Isaiah 31:3)

In Exodus 31: 3-5 Bezaleel received gifts of the **Spirit** so that he understood and had knowledge of various kinds of workmanship. When we move forward to Judges 14: 6 we learn that when a young lion roared against Samson *"... the Spirit of the* ***Lord*** *came mightily upon him, and he tore the lion apart as one would have torn apart a young goat, though he had nothing in his hand. But he did not tell his father or his mother what he had done."* Again, we find that the Spirit empowered Samson but when that **Spirit** left him, he was helpless. What a lesson for us today! (Judges 16: 20 NKJV) It was the word of the Lord to Zerubbabel, *"... Not by might nor by power, but by* ***My Spirit***, *Says the Lord of hosts."* (Zechariah 4:6) It was Isaiah who prophesied of Jesus that, *"The* ***Spirit*** *of the Lord shall rest upon Him, The Spirit of wisdom and understanding. The* ***Spirit*** *of counsel and might. The Spirit of knowledge and of the fear of the Lord."* (Isaiah 11:2) This prophesy was fulfilled at the baptism of Jesus (Matthew 3: 16).

Again, we see the **nature** of the Holy Spirit is that of empowering people for service and ministry. What a blessing!

In the Old Testament, the thing that qualified a prophet to prophesy was that the **Spirit** of the **Lord** would rest upon him (Numbers 11: 25-26). These are recurring themes throughout the Old and New Testament. It is the empowering of the Spirit of God that makes the difference in the life of the man of God. Without that power he is as helpless as was Samson after his disobedience to the Lord. In his prayer of confession, David recognized the necessity of **Holy Spirit** power in his life. He not only pleaded that the Lord would cleanse him of his sin but he pleaded, *"Do not cast me away from Your presence, And do not take Your **Holy Spirit** from me."* (Psalm 51:11) He recognized that only the Holy Spirit could restore him to the joy of the Lord's salvation. It was the prophet Joel who gave the word of the Lord concerning a day in the future when the Lord said, *"…that I will pour out **My Spirit** on all flesh; …"* (Joel 2: 28)

These few passages that we have mentioned are, by no means, an exhaustive study of the work of the Holy Spirit in the Old Testament but they are designed to demonstrate that the person of the Holy Spirit, as a part of the Trinity, has been at work from the beginning of creation even until now.

Can Be Grieved

Another characteristic of the Holy Spirit is that He is sensitive to the needs and the behavior of man. For instance, Paul admonishes believers, *"Do not grieve the **Holy Spirit** of God by whom you were sealed for the day of redemption."* (Ephesians 4: 30) Th is can be done by ungodly behavior such as *"bitterness, and wrath, and anger, and clamor, and evil speaking, and … malice"* (Ephesians 4: 31) In the same passage, Paul admonishes us to *"Be kind to one another, tender-hearted, forgiving one another, just as God in Christ also forgave you."* (Ephesians 4: 32) It is also true, that as a part of the Godhead, it is the **Holy Spirit** who is the guarantor of our salvation. When we were saved after hearing the word of truth, we were *"…sealed with the Holy Spirit of promise."* (Ephesians 1:13) The Holy Spirit will be the, *"guarantee of our inheritance until the redemption of the purchased possession, to the praise of His glory."* (Ephesians 1:14)

Can Be Quenched

The person of the Holy Spirit will not force Himself upon us. While He is sensitive to our needs and our behavior, it is possible for us to "quench" the Spirit. In the closing of the letter to the church at Thessalonica, Paul admonishes the believers that they "... *not quench the Spirit.*" (I Thessalonians 5: 19) This is an awesome thing that man is capable of doing. Therefore, we see that it is God, the Holy Spirit, who convicts us and brings us to salvation (John 3: 5; 16: 13). God, the Holy Spirit, seals our salvation. He provides the "guarantee" or down payment that assures completion of our salvation in the day of the Lord when He shall return and receive us unto Himself.

He Empowers Us

The most important manifestation of the **Holy Spirit** in the history of redemption was His outpouring on the day of Pentecost. It was on that day that the King of Kings through the Spirit empowered His church to do kingdom work. This began the formation of the earthly body of Christ. It is clear, however, that the condition and attitude of the church in the present day has changed drastically. It seems that, in many cases, the presence of the Holy Spirit is absent from the work of the church.

When a Church Grieves the Spirit

The things we are discussing concerning the Holy Spirit often translate into everyday life. An example of the Spirit's absence from the church was revealed when I witnessed the resignation of a young pastor who, admittedly, had made some mistakes in his ministry. I listened as the young man told of his present and continued love for the church. I heard him apologize profusely for those mistakes and ask forgiveness of the congregation. They were not mistakes that would normally call for a resignation. He had not been immoral, unethical or illegal in any of his actions. The congregation proudly announced that he had truthfully proclaimed the Word of God. Then what was the problem? How had this situation degenerated to this point? The explanation from his critics was that he had neglected to visit members who should have been visited and that sometimes he had been argumentative.

As he stood to resign, filled with controlled emotion, he said, "Let me make this clear. I am being forced out and I am not leaving because I want to leave. Some of you have pushed for me to resign and I have no other choice." At that moment there was a very strong sense that the Holy Spirit was grieved. God was sorrowful about the terrible plight of that young pastor. The Holy Spirit of God was grieved because of the abuse and hurt that was visited upon this young pastor and his family.

This situation would never have occurred if the membership of this church had really understood the work, power and presence of the **person** of the **Holy Spirit**. Here is something to think about. Would this church have acted differently had it been under the control of the Holy Spirit? I say, **yes**! This young man would have never found himself in this circumstance had the Holy Spirit been in control of the church. It does not mean that the people of that congregation are not Christians. That may have been true of some, but I was convinced that most of them were misguided Christians. A very small cadre of individuals, who had a gripe because they did not get the pastoral attention they believed they deserved, unduly influenced this congregation. They were unwilling to forgive their Pastor, even though he had sought their forgiveness. Apparently, those antagonists had forgotten the warning of Jesus who said, "... *If you do not forgive men their trespasses, neither will your Father forgive your trespasses.*" (Matthew 6:15) It is a fact that the Holy Spirit is not the author of confusion. When confusion comes to a church, God is not honored and He has no part in it.

The Glory Will Depart

When things of this nature happen, the glory of God often departs from that church. The Word of God speaks to such a time in the life of His people. In Israel, the presence and glory of God was always identified with the Ark of the Covenant. In I Samuel 4, the Holy Spirit inspired the writer to give us an example of the glory departing from the presence of His people. I Samuel 4: 20-22 says, "*and about the time of her death the women who stood by her said to her, 'Do not fear, for you have borne a son.' But, she did not answer, nor did she regard it. Then she named the child Ichabod, saying 'The glory has departed from Israel!' because the ark of God had been captured and because of her father-in-law and her husband. And she said, 'The glory has departed from Israel for the ark of God has been captured.'*" Israel knew the power of God's presence and how they prospered and were strengthened when they faithfully followed the Lord. When Israel made the choice to turn from God, then the presence of God was no longer among them. The glory had departed.

The background to this passage shows Israel making plans to go to battle against the Philistine army. They decided to take the Ark of the Covenant with them into battle because they thought that God would be obligated to give them victory. As the story progresses we see that God did not give them a victory. Israel was defeated and the Philistine army captured the ark and took it away. A messenger came from the battlefield to Eli, who was 98 years of age, with news of defeat, the capture of the ark and the death of his two sons. The news was so shocking to Eli that he fell backward off his chair, broke his neck and died.

One of Eli's daughters-in-law was expecting. When she received the news that her husband, brother-in-law and father-in-law were all dead, she went into labor and a son was born. She died soon after the delivery of the baby. She named her son *"Ichabod,"* which means: *"The glory has departed."* Because of the disobedience of Israel, they were defeated and *"The glory departed from Israel."*

In 1 Samuel 16: 14 we find another example of the Spirit departing. It says, *"But the Spirit of the Lord departed from Saul, and a distressing spirit from the Lord troubled him."* The Lord simply abandoned him to the evil he had embraced. Saul's actions became those of an insane man. Something very similar happened to Nebuchadnezzar who introduced idolatry to the nation and wound up eating grass like an ox (Daniel 4: 31 - 32). The story of Samson, that we have already discussed, is another example of a man who was at one time empowered by the Spirit but there came a time when the **Lord** departed from him. When the Spirit of God departs, circumstances always turn bad. However, there is a solution to the Spirit's departure. God wants His church to succeed. He does not want the church to be defeated and falter in its task. The Word of God has some lessons for us to learn.

Laodicean Complex

Let us heed the words of Jesus when He spoke to the church at Laodicea in Revelation 3: 14-22. The members of the church thought everything was well, but Jesus told them they were *"wretched, and miserable, and poor, and blind, and naked."* In fact, the Spirit of God had left the church and they did not even know it.

Let us look at the passage:

"And to the angel of the church of the Laodiceans write,

These things says the Amen, the Faithful and True Witness, the Beginning of the creation of God: I know your works, that you are neither cold nor hot. I could wish you were cold or hot.

So then, because you are lukewarm and neither cold nor hot, I will spew you out of My mouth.

Because you say, 'I am rich, have become wealthy, and have need of nothing' --and do not know that you are wretched, miserable, poor, blind, and naked --

I counsel you to buy from Me gold refined in the fire, that you may be rich and white garments, that you may be clothed that the shame of your nakedness may not be revealed; and anoint your eyes with eye salve, that you may see.

As many as I love, I rebuke and chasten. Therefore, be zealous and repent.

Behold I stand at the door and knock. If anyone hears My voice and opens the door, I will come in to him and dine with him, and he with Me.

To him who overcomes I will grant to sit with Me on My throne, as I also overcame and sat down with My Father on His throne. He who has an ear, let him hear what the Spirit says to the churches." (Revelation 3: 14-22)

A key element in this text has been overlooked many times.   Jesus says, *"Behold, I stand at the door and knock: ..."* The clear solution is that, *"If any man **hears my voice**, and opens the door, **I will come in.**"*

It is understood by reading what Jesus said that the Spirit can depart and sometimes, He will depart because of the church's neglect of spiritual things. Does that mean He wrote "Ichabod" above the door of the church? The church must realize that the Holy Spirit points us to the Word and the Word is truth (John 17: 17). What the church does with the truth becomes a choice. The church can choose to be obedient or disobedient.

The frightening result of grieving the Holy Spirit is that the power will depart from the church. When this happens, the church can fall into a spiritual malaise and sometimes into a cycle of quarreling dissatisfaction for the rest of the church's existence. This absence of obedience to the truths of the Spirit may result in the loss of interest on the part of many of its members, the loss of respect in the community it is supposed to serve, and eventually the death of the church. Humanly speaking, there is no way to help a church in this condition. Because of the Holy Spirit being quenched and the church beginning to spiral toward death, "well meaning" men try to devise methods to salvage the remnants of the church. At best, their efforts usually fail. The only hope is for the church to regain the presence and power of the **person** of the **Holy Spirit.**

Many churches see the Holy Spirit as a **symbol** of the presence of God revealed in a dove or a flame of fire posted on a denominational placard. Most, when asked about their belief in the Holy Spirit, will be quick to say, "Why of course I believe." The truth is that there is often little belief involved. Many churches seem to have shifted from a dependence on the **Holy Spirit** to a dependence on **human intellect** and belief, thus the result is an ailing church that, like the Laodicean church, does not realize the cause of its illness.

Much of what we see in church quarrels and resulting splits come because of disbelief in the presence and power of the Holy Spirit. It is not easy. The church must deal with this nagging, crippling problem. How can one Christian **gossip** about another Christian if the Holy Spirit is present and alive in his life? How is it that a church can allow **division** and **dissension** to taint the cause of Christ in the community? It is because there is no real dependence **upon** and trust in the power and presence of the **Holy Spirit.**

Changing the way we "do" church will not bring the power and presence of the Holy Spirit into our midst. Accepting the world's ways into the fellowship of believers will never bring the **power** and **presence** of the Holy Spirit. On the contrary, it will bring more problems. If the church is not controlled by the **Holy Spirit,** something or someone else will be in control. The church is made up of people and if those people are not **Spirit filled** then the church will not be **Spirit powered.**

A Seared Conscience

When the local church ceases to operate under the leadership and power of the **person** of the **Holy Spirit** there will be no conscience in the church. When the Holy Spirit departs, there will be a void in the work of that church. There will be no real conviction because the Holy Spirit will not be dealing with the conscience of the church. Apart from the Holy Spirit, man's conscience will not be pricked. There will be no sensitivity to the presence and the leadership of God. As a result, men will do things their own way. Tragically, there are some in the church who exist with a "seared" conscience (1 Timothy 4:2). Another way of speaking of an unpricked conscience is found in Ephesians 4:18-19 when it speaks of those who "*because of the **hardness** of their **heart** become **callous**.*"

The word for the human "conscience" (suneidesis - συνείδησίσ) means to possess "co-knowledge" of something that results in an understanding of guiltiness before God. Literally, a part of us has been instilled by **God** to help us to know right from wrong. A.W. Tozer says that the "secret presence of Christ in the world" is the foundation stone of the human conscience. If the Holy Spirit's power is removed there will be no conviction concerning right or wrong and disastrous things can happen to the church in that vacuum.

We learn from the Scripture that some Christians have "*left their first love" (Jesus)* (Revelation 2: 4). This can result in a seared conscience and a hard heart. If this is true, then we must stop trying to find new ways of "**doing**" church and emphasize **being** the church. This means getting back to our **first love** and back into a right relationship with God. It gets back to the presence and power of the **person** of the **Holy Spirit.**

A Much Needed Mentor

When Jesus ascended from earth, He promised that He would send a comforter. That comforter is the Holy Spirit. He is the church's mentor. "Mentor" literally means, "trusted counselor, guide, tutor or coach". As mentor, He will be with us forever. In fact, He will indwell us. He will teach us. He will uncover the mysteries of the Gospel for us. He produces spiritual character in us (Galatians 5:22-23). As our mentor, He is the church's role model and encourager. However, the main ministry of the Holy Spirit as mentor is to uncover and reveal truth for us and to us. We are reminded again, of what Jesus meant when He said that the Holy Spirit would "*guide you into all truth…*" (John 16:13) He teaches us how to discern what is **right** and what is **wrong**. We cannot get that discernment anywhere else but from the Holy Spirit of God. If left in this world on its own, the church would surely be deceived and fail.

What The Spirit Means To Us

Apart from the Holy Spirit, the church is like a ship without a rudder that is adrift in a raging storm. The **Holy Spirit** provides everything we **need** as a church. He is our teacher and guide concerning truth (John 16:13). He is our intercessor before the throne of God (Romans 8:26-27). The Holy Spirit gives us abundant joy and peace that passes understanding (Philippians 4:7). He gifts us for ministry for the Lord Jesus (Ephesians 4:11-12, 6:17). He provides boldness for witnessing to the lost (1 Timothy 3:13). He gives us power (Zechariah 4:6). He helps us to live Godly lives (Ezekiel 36:27). He helps us to pray (Ephesians 6:18).

The Spirit guides us in doing everything the church needs to do. He produces Christian fruit (Galatians 5:22-23). He provides for Christian service (Ephesians 2:10, Titus 2:14). He produces an atmosphere for worship (Ephesians 5:18-20). He is the source of direction, polity and government in the church. The Lord Jesus is the head of the church as He sits at the right hand of the Father directing the affairs of the church through the Holy Spirit. The Holy Spirit provides, reveals, equips and energizes all the ministries of the church. There is nothing the church needs that the Holy Spirit does not provide. It is a mistake when men seek to improve on what God has already provided by imposing their own ideological concepts of the church in our world.

Summary

A.W. Tozer sums up the whole question of who the Holy Spirit really is and what He does. He clarifies the identity of the Holy Spirit. He makes it clear that the Holy Spirit plays the most significant role in the life of the church. He said, "The Holy Spirit is a person. He is not enthusiasm. He is not courage. He is not energy. He is not the personification of all good qualities, as Jack Frost is the personification of cold weather. Actually, the Holy Spirit is not the personification of anything... He has individuality. He is one being and not another. He has will and intelligence. He has hearing. He has knowledge and sympathy and ability to love, see, and think. He can hear, speak, desire, grieve and rejoice. He is a person." Let's quit treating the Holy Spirit like some unimportant symbol and realize that He, as a part of the God Head, is God with us and because He is with us we need to let Him lead, love, guide and cause us to be more like the Master.

For the church to become Spirit powered it must regain its commitment to the person, presence and power of the Holy Spirit. If we will avail ourselves of Him, we will cease to look for powerless methods concocted in the minds of well meaning men. We do not have to wonder about how to "**do**" church if we will allow the Holy Spirit to help us "**be**" the church.

There will be a fuller discussion of some of these characteristics of the Holy Spirit later in this book. Our purpose here is to establish the fact that the Holy Spirit is a **person** who is a part of the **Godhead**. It is by Him that the energy of the Trinity is dispatched to believers in the world today. The church that first understands these things has taken a bold step toward the status of a **Spirit powered church**.

POINTS FOR DISCUSSION

1. Consider the statement, "The Holy Spirit is not simply a power or an influence. It is essential for a church to understand that the Holy Spirit is a **person**. The Scripture always refers to the Holy Spirit in the masculine gender. He is not only a person but He is the third person of the **Trinity**. He is a part of the Godhead who was active in creation." Discuss why it is so important that we understand the real identity of the Holy Spirit.

2. The Bible says in Judges 14: 6 that when a young lion roared against Samson "... *the Spirit of the **Lord** came mightily upon him, and he tore the lion apart as one would have torn apart a young goat, though he had nothing in his hand. But he did not tell his father or his mother what he had done."* Again, we find that the Spirit empowered Samson but when that **Spirit** left him, he was helpless. What kind of lesson is in the account of Samson for you as a Christian as well as the church today?

3. Paul admonishes believers, *"Do do not grieve the **Holy Spirit** of God by whom you were sealed for the day of redemption."* (Ephesians 4: 30) Ungodly behavior such as *"bitterness, and wrath, and anger, and clamor, and evil speaking, and ... malice"* will grieve the Holy Spirit. Discuss some ways that you think the Holy Spirit can be grieved in your life and your churches life.

4. While He is sensitive to our needs and our behavior, it is possible for us to "quench" the Spirit. In the closing of the letter to the church at Thessalonica, Paul admonishes the believers that they *"... not quench the Spirit."* (I Thessalonians 5: 19) Discuss the difference between **grieving** and **quenching** the Holy Spirit.

5. Is there a Biblical precedent for the glory of God to depart (leave) a church? The Word of God speaks to such a time in the life of His people. In Israel, the presence and glory of God was always identified with the Ark of the Covenant. Read I Samuel 4: 20-22. Do you know of a church where the glory of God has departed? Discuss remedies for the Glory's departure.

6. Discuss the meaning of the word "Ichabod" found in I Samuel 4. Is it possible for "Ichabod" to be written on the life of a church today? If so, how?

7. Discuss the statement made "when the local church ceases to operate under the leadership and power of the **person** of the **Holy Spirit** there will be no conscience in the church." How will this affect personal conviction? Do you agree with the statement, "Apart from the Holy Spirit, man's conscience will not be pricked?" Why or why not?

Step Two
Seek the Spirit's Validation of Our Faith

The first and most important validation of our faith is **Scriptural validation.** A **Spirit** powered people must have an unshakable assurance of their Biblical faith if they are to have a **Spirit powered church.** We must never lose sight of the fact that "*... The natural man does not receive the things of the Spirit of God, for they are foolishness to him; nor can he know them, because they are spiritually discerned.*" *(*I Corinthians 2: 14) In the process of salvation, we are **informed** by the Scripture, **convicted** by the **Spirit** and **saved** by the atonement of Christ at Calvary. Always the Scripture leads to conviction by the Holy Spirit. It was not idle talk when Paul, in writing instructively to young Timothy said, "*and that from childhood you have known the Holy Scriptures, which are able to make you wise for salvation through faith which is in Christ Jesus.*" (II Timothy 3:15) It was in the next verse that Paul wrote, "*All Scripture is given by inspiration of God, and is profitable for doctrine, for reproof, for correction, for instruction in righteousness.*" (verse 16)

That is the reason Christian workers must always use the Scripture in bringing people to faith in Jesus Christ. Personal testimonies are good but they must always be rooted in Scripture. The preacher of the Gospel must always remember that it is not tear jerking stories or sad songs that bring **Holy Spirit** conviction. It is **always** the Scripture. In the book of Ephesians, we are instructed to "*... Take the helmet of salvation, and the sword of the Spirit, which is the Word of God.*" (Ephesians 6: 17) Clearly, we learn from this passage that the Word of God is the tool that is used by the **Holy Spirit** to accomplish His work. In the book of Hebrews, we have a wonderfully assuring declaration that, "*... The word of God is living and powerful, and sharper than any two-edged sword, piercing even to the division of soul and spirit, and of joints and marrow, and is a discerner of the thoughts and intents of the heart.*" (Hebrews 4: 12) The Word of God is a book that is **alive.** It has a life giving nature about it, made possible by the work of the **Holy Spirit.**

The Scriptural Distinctive

The Scriptural distinctive in the life of the Christian is forcefully declared in Romans 8. The writer points out that, "*... what the law could not do in that it was weak through the flesh, God did by sending His own Son in the likeness of sinful flesh, on account of sin: He condemned sin in the flesh, that the righteous requirement of the law might be fulfilled in us who do not walk according to the flesh but according to the **Spirit**.*" *(verses 3 & 4)*

Paul declares that:

"*... Those who live according to the flesh set their minds on the things of the flesh, but those who live according to the **Spirit**, the things of the **Spirit**.*

For to be carnally minded is death, but to be spiritually minded is life and peace.

Because the carnal mind is enmity against God; for it is not subject to the law of God, nor indeed can be.

*So then, those who are in the flesh cannot please God. However, you are not in the flesh but in the **Spirit**, if indeed the **Spirit of God** dwells in you. Now if any man does not have the **Spirit** of Christ, he is not His.*" *(Romans 8: 5 - 8)*

These verses make it clear that salvation is inexorably entwined with the **Holy Spirit**. Salvation is determined by the presence or absence of the **Holy Spirit** in our lives. Regardless of good works, position in life, ritual, talent, or even position in the Church, it is all vain unless it is the work of the **Holy Spirit** in our lives. Antithetically, Paul points out that: "*... If Christ is in you, the body is dead because of sin, but the **Spirit** is life because of righteousness. But if the Spirit of Him who raised Jesus from the dead dwells in you, He who raised Christ from the dead will also give life to your mortal bodies through His **Spirit** who **dwells in you**.*" (Romans 8: 10 - 11) It is clear then, that the one who does possess the indwelling **Holy Spirit** has experienced that wonderfully regenerating salvation that is proffered through Jesus Christ the Son of God!

Regenerate Membership

The church that would be **Spirit powered** must maintain an unwavering insistence on a regenerate membership. Many pastors fear that there is a heart breaking number of lost people on church membership rolls. In fact, sadly enough, many church leaders have never experienced the salvation that can only come because of the convicting, validating power of the Holy Spirit. It is safe to say that there is no salvation apart from the convicting work of the person of the Holy Spirit. Therefore, the salvation of any soul is the proof, the **validation** of the work and power of the Holy Spirit. When the subject of the Holy Spirit comes up, some people always want to talk about supernatural miracles (healing, etc.) while forgetting that the greatest supernatural miracle that ever takes place in a life is the **miracle** of **salvation**. Only the Holy Spirit can convict a lost sinner of the need to be saved. That **validates** the power of the Holy Spirit to **empower the church**. More about this in **Step Five.**

After delivering a sermon on the convicting power of the Holy Spirit, a pastor was surprised to see an elderly woman come forward during the invitation. With obvious brokenness, she said, "Pastor, if what you said today is true, and I believe to be so, then I have never been saved. Today for the first time I have experienced the hand of God upon my life and I am deeply convicted of my sin. I need to be saved!" This woman had been a senior adult women's teacher for decades but she, by her own acknowledgment, had never had a personal relationship with Jesus. She trusted Christ as her Savior and the pastor baptized her the following Sunday morning. Her words of testimony to the congregation were, "Now I know that I'm a child of God. For the first time in my life, I am experiencing the presence and power of the Holy Spirit." I would say that was clear **validation** that the Holy Spirit was at work. The validation of our Christian faith does not get any better than that!

Effects Of The Spirit

We see then, that the indwelling **Holy Spirit** affects everything about us. It affects our attitude toward our fellow man. It affects our behavior. The Christian is not forever having to debate about worldly behaviors because he knows what is right and wrong due to the indwelling **Holy Spirit** in his life. It affects where he places his loyalties. It affects his moral standards. The **Spirit filled** Christian has no hesitancy in heeding the admonition of I Thessalonians 5: 22 to, *"Abstain from every form of evil."* The individual who cares little about the Holy Spirit's influence will live like the rest of depraved humanity.

Many of our young adults simply do not understand the difference between right and wrong. They have no problem with drinking alcohol.

They use the excuse: "Jesus drank wine (which was not fermented and nothing more than grape juice) so there is nothing wrong with me taking a drink now and then." I know of men and women who at one time in their lives abhorred the use of alcohol but now they have a wet bar in their home stocked with various kinds of liquor. What has gone wrong? Do these individuals not understand that their testimony is being destroyed by their behavior? The answer is simple. They do these things because they have a **disconnect with the Holy Spirit**. When there is that disconnect there is no conscience and if there is no conscience, there is no concern with testimony or appearances.

One has only to visit the internet and go on "Face Book" or "You Tube" to observe some of the entries by young adults who say they are Christian. They are seen in pictures proudly holding alcoholic beverages. They appear in these venues half-nude and boast of their sexual indulgences the night before. They brag about all night sessions of illicit sex and they see nothing wrong with their sinful actions. In the absence of the Holy Spirit of God, there is a void and that void causes the individual to care less about appearances. This explains why those Christians who are **Spirit** filled are never the ones who wreak havoc in the body of the church.

Carnality

Carnality was a serious problem in the Corinthian church. Paul said he could not speak to the church because they were no longer spiritual but carnal in every way. It simply means that the **Holy Spirit** was no longer in control. As a result, there was no spiritual growth. In fact, Paul referred to them as "*babes in Christ*" (I Corinthians 3: 1-4). Further, other symptoms of the carnal church were outbreaks of envy and strife. There was still another symptom and that was one of "... *behaving like mere men*." What does that mean? Simply put, they were living like unregenerate people. This church had departed from the presence and power of the Holy Spirit and it was now in shambles. The solution, however, is found in Galatians 5:16, "... *Walk in the **Spirit**, and you **shall not** fulfill the **lust** of the **flesh**.*" Carnality is a problem in present day churches and the only solution is returning to the **Holy Spirit** power that was made available to us when we were **born again**.

Carnality leads to a life of pride and arrogance. These things are always a threat to the unity of any church. Pride does not dwell in the same vessel with the Holy Spirit. Arrogance must flee in the presence of the **Holy**

Spirit. Paul teaches in numerous passages that humility is the way of life for the Spirit filled child of God. There will be no triviality in the church fellowship if pride and arrogance are removed. These twins of evil will flee when the Christian commits to crucifying self daily. Prideful people proclaim boastingly, "This is **my** church." In truth, only **Jesus Christ** can say that about the church. It is truly **His**! When carnal Christians become leaders in the church they always tend to lead the church into carnality, which will destroy a fellowship because it knows no boundaries.

Discernment

The **Spirit powered church** will have the **discernment** to determine who are carnal Christians and who are **Spirit** filled. Any church that is constantly following the leadership of carnal Christians will live in a state of turmoil and the church that learns to shun the bullying and goading of carnal members and follow the leadership of the **Spirit** filled Christians will always accomplish great things in His name. What a validation of faith in Jesus Christ! How critical it is that Christians, in the spirit of Christ, determine that "... *If anyone does not have the Spirit of Christ, he is not His."* (Romans 8: 9) How? Jesus said it well, "*Therefore by their fruits you will know them."* (Matthew 7:20) Galatians 5: 22 & 23 is also an affirmation of the importance of the fruits of the Spirit. More about this in **Step Four**.

The writer of Hebrews, poses that eternal question, "*How shall we escape if we neglect so great a salvation, which at the first began to be spoken by the Lord, and confirmed to us by those who heard him, God also bearing witness both with signs and wonders, with various miracles, and gifts of the **Holy Spirit**, according to His own will?"* (Hebrews 2: 3-4) It was the promise of Jesus Himself to his disciples that when "...*The **Spirit of Truth** has come, He will **guide you into all truth** ..."* (John 16:13) Again, the **Holy Spirit** is active in confirming the great experience of salvation and is listed among the **confirming wonders** of our salvation.

So we see, then, that there is a reason for the declaration of Scripture that, "*all Scripture is given by inspiration of God."* (II Timothy 3: 16) The word "*inspiration*" is translated from the word theopneustos (θεοπνευμστο) which means "God breathed". This confirms to us that the **Holy Spirit,** as a part of the Godhead, is the one who delivered the Scriptures to mankind. It was a special ministry of the **Holy Spirit** that would deliver inspiration to chosen writers until the Word of God was completed. Nothing so authenticates the Scriptures than the knowledge that God, the **Holy Spirit,** was the one who gave the message to those who penned the Scriptures. It literally confirms the fact that the Scriptures are *"God breathed."*

Simon Peter was the preacher on the day of Pentecost. His sermon was laced with Scripture that pricked the hearts of the people gathered there from all over the known world until they cried out, *"What shall we do?"* This message gave Peter's listeners, as well as people today, a more *"sure word"* concerning the Scriptures. He said that: *"Prophecy never came by the will of man, but holy men of God spoke as they were moved by the **Holy Spirit.**"* (II Peter 1: 21) Peter is the one who saw about 3,000 souls saved and added to the church on the day of Pentecost. What a difference it made in their lives! Everything about their lives changed and they *"... continued steadfastly in the apostles' **doctrine** and **fellowship** and in the breaking of bread and in **prayers.**"* (Acts 2: 42) Therefore, this Scripture makes it clear that the **Holy Spirit** communicates to us through the Scripture by teaching us that the Scripture is good for **doctrine,** which tells us what we must believe. We must believe this important truth. It also is good for *"**reproof.**"* This means that the **Holy Spirit** guides us away from heresy and teaches us what we are not to believe. It is good for *"**correction.**"* This means that the Scripture warns us of hurtful things that we are not to do. It also tells us what things will be deceitful and destructive to our testimony. It is also good for our *"**instruction in righteousness**"* which tells us the **Holy Spirit** will guide us into paths of righteousness *"for His namesake."* (Psalm 23)

Unpardonable Sin

We come now to discuss one of the most pivotal Scriptures in the New Testament concerning the work and function of the **Holy Spirit**. We have already discussed the fact that when Jesus cast off the limitations of the flesh and ascended to the right hand of the Father, He promised to send the Comforter who would be **unrestrained** by a body of flesh. The time would pass when the *"... Word became flesh and dwelt among us..."* (John 1: 14) Now the third person of the Trinity would come and minister in the world as the *"**Spirit of Truth**"* who will guide the disciples (some of whom would be writing Scripture) into **all truth**. Jesus made it clear that He (the Holy Spirit) would not speak of Himself but that He would relay to us the message from God the Father and the Son. All things had been committed unto Jesus Christ and the **Holy Spirit** would glorify Christ because He would receive what had been committed unto Christ. In this process, He will "... *convict the world of sin, and of righteousness and of judgment.*" (John 16:8) What does that mean?

Jesus informs us that the **Holy Spirit** will convict the world of the most grievous **sin** that anyone can commit: "... ***Because they did not believe in Me.***" (verse 9) Many have wondered and been confused as to what it is to commit sin against the Holy Spirit or the unpardonable sin. Some have thought that it was to commit murder. Murder is a grievous sin. However, murder is not a sin that cannot be forgiven. It is not drunkenness or immorality, although these are very grievous sins. The **sin of unbelief** is the sin against the **Holy Spirit**. This one sin will send an individual to an eternal Hell. It does not matter how many good works one has done, without **belief** in Jesus Christ, our Savior, there is no hope in eternity for anyone, regardless of one's station in life. Jesus made it clear that "... *Whosoever speaks against the **Holy Spirit**, it will not be forgiven him, either in this age or in the age to come.*" (Matthew 12: 32) Th e same Jesus stated emphatically that, "... *Every sin and blasphemy will be forgiven men, but the blasphemy against the **Spirit** will not be forgiven men.*" (verse 31) Why? Because the **Holy Spirit** is the one who draws us to Christ. When one rejects His convicting power there is no other **approach to the Savior.** Th is sin is sometimes manifested in the life and ministry of the local church.

One Sunday morning after the service, a frail little woman approached the pastor asking, "Pastor, will you come and visit my husband? I have witnessed to him for years without success. He might hear you." Of course, the pastor agreed. The next day the pastor visited the man. He was friendly and cordial while the pastor shared the plan of salvation with him. Then the pastor asked if he would like to accept Jesus Christ as His Lord and Savior. The man tearfully responded, "Preacher, you don't understand, God will not save me. My life has been too sinful. I have turned away and rejected God too many times. He would never save me." The Pastor realized, because of the man's own testimony, that it was futile to carry on the conversation. Later that year the man died. He was never saved.

Tragic? To be sure it was. However, the reality is that many will not believe in the saving power of Christ. Here is a question. Was it his sin that caused him to be lost or was it his belief that God would not save him that caused him to be lost? In the end, his sin against the Holy Spirit was that of rejecting Jesus Christ. Jesus, Himself, warned about this sin in the Sermon on the Mount when He said, "*Enter by the narrow gate; for wide is* the gate and broad is the way that leads to destruction, and there are **many** who go in by it." (Matthew 7:13)

Nicodemus

One night, in a conversation with Nicodemus, Jesus gave a companion teaching. He assured Nicodemus that he must be born again. Nicodemus had difficulty understanding how this could be. He asked if a man could enter a second time into his mother's womb and be born. That is a reference to the physical birth. The answer of Jesus was, "... *Unless one is born of water (physical birth) and the Spirit, he cannot enter into the kingdom of God.*" (John 3: 5) Here Jesus, Himself, stresses the vital function of the **Holy Spirit** in the salvation experience. He compared the **Spirit** to the blowing of the wind when He said, "*The wind blows where it wishes, and you hear the sound of it, but cannot tell where it comes from and where it goes. So is everyone who is born of the **Spirit**.*" (Verse 8)

Like the Wind

The New Birth has a certain mystery about it. It is especially mysterious when we try to understand it in its entirety. Ray C. Stedman calls the experience "the exchanged life." He says, "This is the secret of a Christian: he is not living his own life, he is living another's life. Or, more accurately, another is living his life in him." This is a perfect picture of the experience of salvation and the indwelling of the Holy Spirit.

We do not really understand the mystery about the **spiritual** birth just as we do not understand everything about the wind. Jesus is saying that is the way it is when we are born of the **Spirit**. The wind has many functions in the world. It will drive a great ship at sea. It will generate electricity but it can be destructive in a tornado. It can also come as a gentle breeze that cools us on those hot summer evenings. Even so, the **Spirit** has many functions that we will discuss later. This kind of birth happens to us because "*God so loved the world.*" (John 3: 16) He further assures Nicodemus that "... *God did not send His Son into the world to condemn the world, but that the world through Him might be saved.*" (John 3: 17) Then Jesus gives that great clincher line when He said, "*He who believes in Him is not condemned; but he who does not believe is condemned already, because he has not **believed in the name of the only begotten Son of God**.*" (John 3: 18) That is the sin against the **Holy Spirit**.

Here again, we see the triune God at work in our salvation and the operative word is **believe**. There is no need for any **believer** to worry about whether or not he has committed sin against the **Holy Spirit**. It is clear from the Scripture that the sin against the **Holy Spirit** is a **final** and **complete** rejection of Jesus Christ. No one who believes in Jesus Christ has committed the sin against the Holy Spirit, and he will never be condemned! It does not mean that a person who has simply **procrastinated** as the **Holy Spirit** has convicted, has sinned against the **Spirit** but it does mean that the person who repeatedly rejects the prompting of the **Spirit** will be less and less sensitive to the urging of the **Spirit.** It is as though the law of **diminishing returns** sets in. One can so quench the **Spirit** and the **Spirit** is so grieved that one becomes seared and calloused toward God. It is a condition of the mind, soul and spirit that is hostile against the prompting of the Holy Spirit that only God can judge. One person should never tell another that he has committed the unpardonable sin. Man must never go beyond what the Scripture clearly teaches. The book of Hebrews tells us of a time when this happened to Esau (Hebrews 12: 16 & 17; Genesis 25: 30-34; Genesis 27: 30-40). Esau despised his birthright and sold it for a mess of stew. As a result, he sinned away his day of grace. Even though he sought the blessing of his birthright with tears, it was too late. His birthright was a **spiritual** thing that he despised. A similar thing happened to Judas who walked with the Lord and had every opportunity, yet he betrayed the Lord. There came that moment when Jesus said to Judas, *"What you do,* do quickly.*"* (John 13:27) The Bible tells us that Judas went out immediately after receiving the sop from Jesus, *"and it was night"* (verse 30). It was **night** in his mind. It was **night in his soul. It** was **night forever** for Judas. It was as though Jesus was saying to Judas, *"**This is it** for you. Make your choice **now** and **that choice is for eternity.**"* Jesus said it would have been better for him if he had never been born (Matthew 26: 24). The apostles said he went to his *"own place"* (Acts 1: 26) indicating that Judas was, indeed a devil just as Jesus said he was (John 6:7). Then there are those sad occasions when one rebels and lashes out against the **Spirit's** conviction. It is a terrible thing when the **Spirit** ceases to deal with the lost soul because of that soul's rejection of Him. J.A. Alexander said it well:

"There is a time, we know not when,
A point we know not where,
That marks the destiny of men

31

To glory or despair.
There is a line by us unseen,
That crosses every path;
The hidden boundary between
God's patience and His wrath.
To pass that limit is to die --
To die as if by stealth; …"

Not only does the Holy Spirit convict the world of the sin of unbelief, but also, He convicts the world of **righteousness** because Jesus returned to the right hand of the Father. Since Jesus returned to the Father, the Spirit guides men in determining what is right and wrong. Therefore, the Scripture does not need to list every sin of every age for the Christian because the **Holy Spirit** so guides the believer that he readily discerns what is destructive to the **Spirit filled** life and the work of the Kingdom of God.

The **Spirit,** moreover, convicts the world of **judgment** because the prince of this world was judged and defeated through the **death** of Christ at Calvary and His **resurrection** from the grave. It is in this way that we understand what Jesus meant when He said, "*I will no longer talk much with you, for the ruler of this world is coming, and he has nothing in Me.*" (John 14: 30) When Jesus was moving toward His crucifixion He declared, "*Now is the judgment of this world; now the ruler of this world will be cast out.*" (John 12: 31) We understand these things now because of the work of the **Holy Spirit.** Thus, we see again that the Scriptural validation of our faith is sound and sure.

Cosmological Validation

There is no function of the **Holy Spirit** that so validates our faith as the cosmological validation or observation of the world about us. It is the testimony of **creation** that many Christian scholars advocate. The work of the **Spirit** is often associated with **light** in the Bible. Right after the **Spirit** "*… was hovering over the face of the waters,*"(Genesis 1: 2) the triune God said, "*… Let there be **light** and there was **light**.*" (Genesis 1:3) It was because, in the fiat creation of the Universe, "*The earth was without form, and void; and **darkness** was on the face of the deep…*" *(*Genesis 1: 2*)* The triune God said that **light** was good. It was the psalmist who said, "*The entrance of Your words gives **light**; It gives understanding to the simple.*"

32

(Psalm 119: 130) David declared, "*The Lord is my **light** and my salvation; Whom shall I fear? The Lord is the strength of my life; Of whom shall I be afraid?*" (Psalm 27:1) David also declared, "*The heavens declare the glory of God; And the firmament shows His handiwork. Day unto day utters speech, And night unto night reveals knowledge.*" (Psalms 19: 1-2). In fact, this Psalm is one of the most moving declarations of the greatness, the power, the justice and the mercy of a triune God to be found anywhere.

The great prophet Isaiah called upon his people to "*… come and let us walk in the light of the Lord.*" (Isaiah 2: 5) In his great Messianic prophecy, he said, "*The people who walked in **darkness** have seen a great **light**; Those who dwelt in the land of the shadow of death, Upon them a **light** has shined.*" (Isaiah 9: 2) Why could Isaiah say this? Because the Lord had given him a vision of things to come which he expressed in verse 6 of Chapter 9: "*For unto us a child is born, unto us a son is given: and the government shall be upon his shoulder: and his name shall be called **Wonderful**, **Counselor**, the **Mighty God**, the **Everlasting Father**, the **Prince of Peace**.*" (Isaiah 9: 6) It was the same great prophet who heard the word from the Lord saying, "*… I will also give You as a **light** to the Gentiles, That You should be My salvation to the ends of the earth.*" (Isaiah 49: 6) The light of God would come from Israel and the theme of the suffering servant was, of course, Jesus Christ the Savior of men. Many Scriptures in the Old Testament identify the work of the **Holy Spirit** with **light**. Darkness is associated with **evil, ignorance, hopelessness** or **chaos**.

Often in the life of the church "**light**" needs to be shed on a particular situation. The idea of "**light**" in this context is simply that of revelation. Many things are revealed to the modern church through the **light** of the Holy Spirit. Works of Satan can be revealed. Sins of the people can be revealed. Lostness can be revealed. The **light** of the **Holy Spirit** shines on the sinfulness of man. The hymn "Holy Spirit, Light Divine" says it well:

"Holy Spirit, light divine,
Dawn upon this soul of mine;
Let your word dispel the night,
Wake my spirit, clear my sight."

The Holy Spirit as "light" will teach us to identify and hate sin and as a result will cause us to cease from blatant sinning. Of course, the metaphor of light in the Bible is derived from the natural Sun.

New Testament

In the first chapter of John, after he concludes his account of creation and the involvement of Jesus in it, he proceeds to tell us about the **true light**. He declares, "*This man came for a witness, to bear witness of the **Light**, that all through him might believe.*" (John 1: 7) In the following verse, John makes it clear that John the Baptist was not that **light** but was sent to bear witness of that **light**. He defines that light as the **true light** that, "*... was the true **Light** which gives **light** to every man who comes into the world.*" *(*John 1: 9*),* and he declares that, "*He was in the world, and the world was **made** through Him and the world did not know Him.*" *(John 1: 10)*

At the transfiguration of Jesus, the Bible says, "*... His **face** shone like the **sun**, and His clothes became as white as the **light**.*" (Matthew 17: 2) When God spoke to them, they were overshadowed by a "*bright cloud.*" The voice of God came from the cloud. The command of God was that Jesus was God's "*... beloved **Son**, in whom I am well **pleased**. **Hear Him**!*" (Matthew 17:5)

Conversion of Paul

In the book of Acts we have the record of a young man named Saul who stood by the coats of those who stoned Stephen and saw a righteous man stoned to death who was "*... full of the **Holy Spirit**, ...*" (Acts 7:55) He gave his life in fidelity to the Lord Jesus while looking into Heaven and seeing the glory of God and the Lord Jesus standing at the right hand of God. Later, Saul unleashed great persecution against the church and was on his way to Damascus with letters from the high priest to bring believers, bound, back to Jerusalem for trial. As he approached Damascus, a great **light** shone around about him and he fell to the ground. The light was so bright that it blinded him for a period of three days. In that experience, he asked two questions that every man must face. One was "*...Who are You, Lord?*" (Acts 9: 5) The other was "*.... Lord, what do You want me to do?*" *(*Acts 9: 6*)* He went to the street called Straight to the house of one named Judas. The Lord sent a believer by the name of Ananias to minister to him. While he heard the voice of Jesus in the midst of the bright **light**, he apparently did not see a form but there is no doubt that Jesus appeared in that **light** and spoke to Saul on the Damascus Road.

The Point

The point is this. We have established that the **Holy Spirit** has been active in the establishment of the physical universe. The most important part of the physical universe is the **sun**. It releases the **energy** that sustains the world. The **Holy Spirit,** from the beginning, was that source through which the energy was released. There is no massive generator that keeps the sun going. The heavens really do declare the glory of **God** (Psalms 19:1). There is no reason for anyone to doubt the existence of God. We can arise each morning and see the beauty of the **sunrise** and in the evening we can see the beauty of the **sunset** and know that the triune God is alive, a lover of beauty, and in charge of this universe. The Scripture is replete with teachings that the **triune God** is behind the energy of the universe that causes flowers to bloom, trees to grow and seed to germinate.

All of this happens by the energy of the sun. The mystery that we call *"photosynthesis"* is an activity of **sunlight** on plant life. If there were no sun, the earth would be darkened. The rivers of the earth, its arteries, would turn to ice. Nothing would grow. The earth could not sustain any kind of life and the sun itself is the most obvious and **daily reminder** of the mighty power of God. It is the **Holy Spirit**, the third person of the triune God, who ushered in and daily administers these things as Genesis 1: 2 & 3 clearly teaches. Thus, **light** has always been associated with the **Holy Spirit**. Any intelligent person can look about him in the universe and know that God is real and that He is alive. Of course, we do not worship nature as pagans sometimes do, but we worship the living **God of nature** who **sustains it** (Colossians 1: 17). It was well established by Jesus himself that He would send the Comforter, the same **Spirit** of Genesis 1, whom He sent on the day of Pentecost to birth the church and empower the church. Many of us Christians have witnessed revival and renewal come to churches when the **Holy Spirit** has sway and the people of the church freely receive the power of the **Holy Spirit**, allowing Him in His power to validate their faith. In fact, revival comes no other way! How could any church not seek the mighty creative power of the **Holy Spirit** whose work can be so **readily observed**?

Nature's Witness

This is what Paul was getting at when the people of Lystra tried to name him and Barnabas after pagan gods. They *"called Barnabas, Jupiter and Paul, Mercurius."* Then the priest of Jupiter brought oxen and garlands into the City to make sacrifice. When Paul and Barnabas heard of it, they were so distressed that they rent their clothes and ran in among the people crying out *"... Men, why are you doing these things? We also are men with the same nature as you, and preach to you that you should turn from those **vain things** to the **living God**, who **made the heaven, the earth, the sea**, and all things that are in them."* (Acts 14:15) Paul is making it clear that the living God is creator of **all things** even though He has *"... allowed all nations to walk in their own ways."* (Acts 14: 16) Paul points out, however, that God *"... did not leave Himself without witness, in that He did good, gave us rain from **heaven** and **fruitful seasons**, filling our hearts with **food** and **gladnes**s."* (Acts 14: 17) Paul is faithfully declaring to them that pagan gods did not provide the bounty of nature to them as they supposed, but the living God provided them and the activity of nature about them was a **witness** to the living **God!** What **validation!**

Many Christian outdoorsmen will attest to the fact that the Holy Spirit is constantly reminding us of what a wonderful creation we live in. There is nothing quite like sitting in a tree stand on a deer hunt and watching the world wake up. First, there is darkness and absolute silence. A cricket will chirp, then another and another. Meanwhile, the birds begin to awaken and flutter from one branch to another. By this time, the sun is rising and everything in the woods comes to life. The presence and power of the person of the Holy Spirit is real in nature and nature is surely a validation of the handiwork of God in this world. Sometimes nature becomes the source of the wrath of God upon sinful man. Even then, the Holy Spirit of God is a real presence. However, it must be understood that the nature we enjoy is the creation and not the creator. Again, it is not God. It is the **handiwork** of God.

God's Wrath

Paul takes it further in Romans 1: 18-24 in pointing out that *"The wrath of God is **revealed** from heaven against all ungodliness and unrighteousness of men who **suppress the truth** in unrighteousness, because what may be **known** of God is **manifest** in them, for God has shown it to them."* (Romans 1: 19) How did God show it to them? Here again we see the effect of *"... the true Light which gives light to **every man** who comes into the world."* (John 1: 9) It is an intuitive knowledge of God that is in the heart and mind of every man. While we have the commission from our Lord to *"... preach* *the gospel to every creature.*" (Mark 16:15) Even men who never hear the explicit gospel will be held accountable for the light they have (see John 9:41; Luke 12: 47 & 48). The message of Romans 1: 19-21 is, "... *What may be known of God **is manifest in them**, for God has shown it to them. For since the creation of the world His invisible attributes are clearly seen, being understood by the **things that are made**, even His **eternal power and Godhead**, so that they are without excuse, because, although they **knew God**, they did not glorify Him as **God**, nor were thankful, but became futile in their thoughts, and their **foolish hearts** were **darkened**.*"

What is a foolish heart? A foolish heart is the heart of a **fool**. Well does the Scripture say, "*the **fool** has said in his heart, 'There is **no God**.' ...*" (Psalm 14: 1) This is not a classification that **Christians** have given. God has given the classification! The atheist has "*in his heart*" and by his own volition **chosen** that designation for **himself**. So, why do some Christians spend so much time arguing with atheists? When are we going to stop referring to them as "bright", "brilliant" or "intelligent" when the **Scripture** says of them, "*professing to be **wise**, they became **fools**.*" (Romans 1:22) Why? Because they "... *changed the glory of the incorruptible **God** into an image made like corruptible man - and birds and four footed beasts, and creeping things.*" (Romans 1: 23) What was God's judgment? He "... ***gave them up** to uncleanness in the lusts of their heats, to dishonor their **bodies** among **themselves**.*" (Romans 1: 24) Who has not heard of the "homosexual rights" people and "animal rights" groups (see Romans 1: 25 - 35)? These Scriptures are being **fulfilled** before our **very eyes**.

Ultimate Condition

This is the ultimate condition of those who reject the **witness** of **creation,** which everywhere gives evidence that the world about us was **created** by the triune God and that He is still in control (Colossians 1: 16 & 17)! That truth is a powerful **validation of our faith**! Christians, therefore, should spend their time bearing witness to a lost world. Some fanatical organizations want to deny humans the use of energy that **God** has placed in the ground for our use. They would deny us the use of the timber that is needed for our shelter to protect some bird, fish or four-footed beast (Romans 1: 23). When this happens energy becomes wildly expensive, housing becomes unaffordable, food supplies are short and prices are inflated; all because of some **foolish** and pagan ideas of fanatics. Christians should use the resources that **God** has given us and understand that the **"green"** movement is not a **God** movement. Many times Christians, especially young ones, are drawn into these fanatical movements under the pretense of "going green." They finally learn that some of the people who head these movements and who are behind them are willing to use Christians but those same people have little use for Christianity in their own lives.

Christians should not allow themselves to be duped by these people because their so-called "environmentalism" becomes a kind of **pagan religion**. Of course, Christians for many decades have been involved in things like soil conservation, water conservation, wildlife conservation and reforestation but it does not become a religion to them. They realize the truth of Genesis 1: 26 that God has placed these things on earth for our good and that man should *"... have **dominion** over the fish of the sea, over the birds of the air, and over the cattle, over all the earth and over every creeping thing that creeps on the earth."* It is a pronouncement of the triune God that man has the intelligence, the emotion and the volition to have dominion over God's Creation. Christians must always understand that they do not fulfill the **Great Commission** (Matthew 28:19) by "going green." The "animal rights" movement sometimes borders on worship of the **creature** more than the **creator**. Moreover, many of the claims, charges and accusations of these movements have proven to be **scientifically** and **factually** a hoax. Many times the movement has fanatical leaders who are not inclined to listen to reason and some openly proclaim themselves to be atheists.

The frightening thing is that many evangelical and mainline Christians are falling into this "going green" trap and the PETA (People for the Ethical Treatment of Animals) pattern to the point of fanaticism. The average church member does not understand what these fanatical organizations propagate. Many do not even know that the majority of these people couldn't care less about the unborn child. In fact, most of them are "pro-choice" when it comes to abortion and birth control. This is such an inconsistency! The Bible teaches that the unborn **child** is just that a **child**. Putting it more bluntly, that unborn child is a living soul. That cannot be said about a bird, a dog, a rabbit or any other living creature. Humans, even the unborn ones, are products of a Holy God. The **Holy Spirit** was present when this earth was created and therefore He is ever mindful of how foolish the world has become concerning such matters.

It Is Time

Is it not time for Christians to stand tall and say to our young people, "Enough! Carl Sagan is wrong! The cosmos is not all there **ever was**, it is not all there **is** and it is not all there ever **will be**. There is a living God who created it all and who sustains it all!" Is it not time to say a resounding, "Yes, Mr. Sagan there is evidence of God aplenty all around you if you could only see and understand it?" Isn't it time to say, "Bill Maher is wrong?" Having a TV program and making a movie does not make him right. There is a God. Maher only reveals to us how shallow some program directors can be. Isn't it time to say, "Enough is enough."? A hospice chaplain, Mirta Signorelli, in Boca Raton, Florida was ordered by her supervisors not to mention the name of God, Jesus Christ or Lord in her public speeches. Isn't it time to say, "Christopher Hitchens is wrong? There is a God and becoming a reporter doesn't qualify him to say there isn't." Isn't it time to tell our young people that Richard Dawkins is wrong? Being a British scholar does not confer upon him any authenticity in declaring that there is no God.

Yes, it is time to say that Charles Darwin is wrong! Even though discoveries in the science of **information** and DNA have totally discredited the evolutionary hypothesis, there are some who still cling to the nonsense that so confuses our youth. Man is not the product of some one celled amoeba or a paramecium that came out of some primeval scum. Man did not evolve from some lower form of animal life. Jesus settled the question once and for all, when He answered the Pharisees by saying: "… *Have you not read that He who made them at the beginning made them **male** and female, …?*" (Matthew 19:4) Jesus was right there in the beginning. He participated in creation with the Father and the Holy Spirit. He was there when God breathed into man the breath of life and He "*became a living soul.*" When did it all happen? *"In the beginning"*. Some desperate evolutionist always asks, "If there is a God could He not have done it all through evolution?" The answer is, "Yes." Of course, God **could** have done anything He wanted to do but He **did** what He **said** He did and God said that He created man as well as all the "beasts of the field." The idea of the survival of the fittest was always nonsense. Nothing was "fitter" than the dinosaurs but they are **gone** (Job 40:15-24; 41:11-34). Yes, there are some similarities between man and some animals because there was a common creator but similarities do not mean that one species came from the other. Jesus never even hinted that we evolved from some form of lower life.

Investigate!

Parents should more thoroughly investigate where they send their children to school. Too many Christian parents are working, scrimping and saving to send their children to college where they are sometimes more brainwashed than educated. Christians never need to bow our heads in shame in face of the arguments from those who would discredit our belief in God and the value of the church in the modern day. Yes, some skeptics are ready to pronounce the church of Jesus Christ as **dead** and it is happening all around us. Yes, it is true that Americans who claim a belief in God has decreased by ten percent in the last decade but the **church is far from dead**. We can be assured that the church is alive forevermore and *"The gates of Hades will not prevail against it."* (Matthew 16:18b)

God has never used huge numbers but He has always used unusual dedication. Gideon's army was downsized before they were ready to accomplish what God wanted them to accomplish. To be sure, there **is** a lot of **evil** and **crime** in the world. This writer, as we mentioned in the introduction, once served as a Chaplain at a state institution for serious juvenile offenders. There were juveniles at that facility who had committed first-degree murder, first-degree rape, armed robbery, carjacking, arson and other crimes. Christians are not committing these terrible crimes. I never found one of them who had a Sunday School attendance pin. They mostly came from broken homes. The few who had ever gone to church were usually taken to church by a Godly Grandmother. If they knew **who** their Father was, they did not know **where** he was. Churches in the area came and taught Sunday School for us. They conducted Bible studies for us and ministered in many ways to the students. The most unsuccessful staff member I ever met was a psychologist who was an atheist whom we were never able to win to faith in Jesus Christ. One student asked, "Chaplain, how can she help me when her own life is a mess?" The life answer was simple. The students who got in touch with God while they were there made it when they were released. A number of those who found Christ as their Savior are now in the ministry. Those who refused the gospel and who never got in touch with God usually turned up in the penal system in some other place. Some were even returned to the facility. Yes, the **Holy Spirit** still works! He still makes a difference!

Time To Be Careful

Again, this is an appeal to Christian parents to take more interest in what your children are being taught in school. Look more carefully at the college or university where you send your child. Parents should seek the guidance of the **Holy Spirit** when choosing schools for their children. One pastor shared his experience and disappointment when a young woman from his church went off to a "Christian" college. On a first visit back home, she was upset. On her first day in religion class, the professor posed the question: "Did **God** create **man** or did **man** create **God**?" His thesis was that man created God. Another Pastor tells of a young man from his church who attended a state university where he encountered a Professor who said, "There is no God and Jesus is His Son."

It is David Horowitz and Jacob Laksin who point out in their recent book, <u>One Party</u> <u>Classroom</u>, that Duke University now offers courses in **Marxism and Society**. One can earn a "certificate" in Marxism by taking six courses chosen from such offerings as "Soviet Literature," "Third World Culture," and "The Chinese Revolution." Marx was an atheist who penned the "Communist Manifesto" (1848). Duke is usually listed among the top ten universities in the nation. Devout Methodist people founded the school for the propagation of the Christian Faith. Of course, Duke is not the only church related college where this sort of thing happens. This is only one example that could be repeated many times over. These examples are shared here only to say that it is time for Christians to be more careful about schools they send their children to and get on the offense about our faith without being offensive.

Yes, it is time for Christians to boldly instruct our young in the ways of God and make sure they are **grounded in their faith** before they leave their homes. However, it may be instructive to hear a statement that Dr. George W. Truett reportedly made when he said, *"It is not my duty to argue with the last fool who has escaped from the mortar in which he was brayed."* (See Proverbs 27:22) There is an admonition of Scripture that says, *"Answer not a fool according to his folly, lest thou also be likened to him."* (Proverbs 16:4) The Scripture has some good advice: *"Do not speak in the hearing of a fool, for he will despise the wisdom of your words."* (Proverbs 23: 9) Usually, atheistic fanatics will not listen to reason but we certainly **can** prepare our young people to deal with atheistic propaganda when they encounter it. This is another reason we need **Spirit** powered churches to nurture our youth and ground them in the faith!

41

Give an Answer

While young Christians should not be given to *"... disputes over doubtful things"* (Romans 14:1) or *"useless wranglings of men of corrupt minds and destitute of the truth ..."* (I Timothy 6: 5) The young Christian should, nevertheless, *"... always be ready to give a **defense** to everyone who asks you a reason for the hope that is in you, with meekness and fear; having a good conscience, that when they defame you as evildoers, those who revile your good conduct in Christ may be ashamed."* (I Peter 3: 15-16) It is the charge of Jude 3 that we *"... should earnestly contend for the faith which was once for all delivered to the saints."*

There are those who have a special calling and a gift to debate with those who would discredit the Christian faith. The apostle Paul was a man with such a gift. At Athens his spirit was stirred within him. When he saw the city wholly given to idolatry, the Scripture says: *"... His spirit was provoked within him when he saw that the city was given over to idols. Therefore he **reasoned in the synagogue** with the Jews and with the Gentile worshipers, and in the marketplace daily with those who happened to be there."* (Acts 17: 16-17) In this case, he was debating with people who obviously had heard little about Jesus Christ.

When Paul arrived at Ephesus, he found a small band of Christians who had believed but knew nothing of the **Holy Spirit**. They had only been baptized with the baptism of John. Paul instructed them that John came with the baptism of repentance but pointing to the One who would come **after** him who was Jesus Christ. When these twelve men heard this, they were baptized in the name of Jesus Christ. Paul laid hands on them and they received the **Holy Spirit**. After this, Paul went into the synagogue where he disputed and persuaded for three months but those in the synagogue were hardened against his message. Then he went to the school of Tyrannus and disputed (debated) where he continued for two years. While the work at Ephesus was difficult in the beginning there came a time, through the ministry of Paul that, *"the name of the Lord Jesus was **magnified**"* and *"mightily grew the word of God and **prevailed**."* The church at Ephesus grew so much that the silversmiths, led by Demetrius, caused a riot because they feared that their trade was in jeopardy. They made silver shrines for the Goddess Diana (Acts 19: 6-41). While Paul did have a gift of debating and persuading, others, men such as Barnabas, did not seem to possess that gift. Jesus' warning was that man should not *"cast your pearls before swine."* (Matthew 7:6)

We will further discuss special callings in the next chapter. The lesson here is to avoid endless arguing or disputing with people who have no desire to really know the truth of the gospel but always be ready to give an answer for our faith and to do that we must be **well grounded** in the **faith**. Debating the faith with those who would destroy it in the battle for the minds of men should be left to those who have a special calling and gift for that ministry.

Validation of Prayer

Wireless communication has been used for centuries. It is called prayer! Prayer is the most personal and indispensable validation of our faith through the ministry of the **Holy Spirit** in our lives. It was the Lord, himself, who said, *"If you then, being evil, know how to give good gifts to your children, how much more will your heavenly Father give the **Holy Spirit** to those who ask Him!"* (Luke 11: 13) Jesus made it clear for time and eternity that the **Holy Spirit** is ours for the **asking**. The **Holy Spirit** is not just a random act of God but He is available to **everyone** who asks for Him. The assurance that God hears our prayers is found in both the Old and New Testaments. When Moses was standing beside the burning bush, the Lord said to him, *"... I have surely seen the oppression of My people who are in Egypt, and have **heard their cry** because of their taskmasters, for I know their sorrows."* (Exodus 3: 7)

For the church, the Holy Spirit is the "Spirit of prayer." There are numerous passages in the Scripture that refer to Him as the "Spirit" of prayer. Paul makes clear references to the Holy Spirit concerning this matter in several passages. In Galatians 4:6, he says *"... God has sent forth the **Spirit** of His Son into your hearts, crying out, **'Abba Father'**!"* Then in Romans 8:15 he says, *"For you did not receive the spirit of bondage again to fear, but you received the **Spirit** of **adoption** by whom we cry out, 'Abba Father'."* As a result, He helps us pray. We do not have to pray ignorantly or with a multitude of words but under the power of the Holy Spirit. The **Spirit powered church** will allow Him to be the "Spirit of prayer." This is the weakest link in church fellowship. It is clear that the Holy Spirit is left out of church life when prayer becomes a task, a rote formality or a burden rather than a joy.

Answered Prayer

In Genesis 18, we have the account of Abraham praying for Abimelech and his household. God healed them (Genesis 20:17). There are many references in the Old Testament revealing the prayer life of kings and prophets. Among those that stand out is the prayer of Elijah on Mount Carmel in the contest with the prophets of Baal. When the prophets of Baal totally failed Elijah prayed to God saying, *"Hear me, O Lord, hear me, that this people may know that You are the Lord God, and that You have turned their hearts back to You again. Then the fire of the Lord fell and consumed the burnt sacrifice, and the wood and the stones and the dust, and it licked up the water that was in the trench."* (I Kings 18: 37-38) In that moment the Lord sent fire from heaven upon the altar of sacrifice and even dried up the water that was running in the trenches around the altar. The response was that the people fell on their faces before God and began to cry, *"The Lord, He is God! He is God!"* (I Kings 18: 39) There is the inspiring account of prayer in the ministry of Elisha who went to the home of the Shunammite woman whose son was dead. Elisha prayed unto the Lord, then he stretched himself upon the child and the child sneezed seven times and was alive (II Kings 4: 32-37).

We could mention the prayer life of King David, especially his prayer of repentance in Psalm 51. Other memorable examples are to be found in the prayer lives of such greats as Jeremiah, Isaiah and Daniel.

The Prayer Life of Jesus

The greatest validation of prayer in the Christian life comes from the prayer life of Jesus. The disciples wanted to pray like Jesus but they never heard Him leading a conference on prayer, nor did He ever write a book on prayer. Prayer to Him was not a psychological classification or a philosophical discourse. It was the Son of God praying and claiming it as His source of power. Prayer was an integral part of the life of Jesus. A Christian's faith will be validated by their prayer life. Prayer opens the door for the Holy Spirit to empower the life of Christians and guide their actions day by day.

During His ministry, Jesus prayed **all night** at times. For instance, the night before He selected His disciples, He went up into a mountain and continued all night in prayer. When it was day, He called His disciples unto Him and choose twelve (Luke 6:12). Jesus also prayed in the **mornings**.

After His baptism and temptation, Jesus returned to Galilee to preach the gospel of the kingdom where He taught in the synagogue and healed the mother-in-law of Simon Peter. Jesus spent a hard day healing many who were sick. Early the next **morning** Jesus rose up, "*... a long while before daylight, He went out and departed to a solitary place; and there He prayed.*" (Mark 1: 35) It was a day when He would be on an evangelistic tour of Galilee. Jesus prayed **before meals**. Just before He distributed the five loaves and two fish, "*... He looked up to heaven, blessed and broke the loaves, and gave them to His disciples .... .*" (Mark 6:41) The practice of praying before meals continues among Christians until this day. Spirit filled Christians are loathe to begin eating a meal without giving thanks unto God before they begin. This is one of the most effective ways to train up our children in the nurture and admonition of the Lord. When we walk into a restaurant or a cafeteria and see Christians bowing to pray before their meal, it tells a lot about their devotion and about the power of the **Holy Spirit** in their lives. If a parent could leave their children millions of dollars, it would not be as helpful to them as teaching them to pray.

Jesus had **evening prayer**. After the task of feeding the five thousand, the Bible says, "*... When He had sent them away, He departed unto a mountain to pray.*" (Mark 6:46) After He had spent time in prayer, He came walking on the water, a memorable event that will never be forgotten. The disciples thought that they had seen a spirit but He spoke to them and said, "*.... Be of good cheer! It is I; do not be afraid.*" (Mark 6:50)

Jesus often sought **solitude** when He prayed. After the miracle of Simon catching a large number of fish at Jesus' command when he had caught nothing all night and after the healing of a leper, Jesus, "*... withdrew into the wilderness and prayed.*" (Luke 5: 16) As we read the ministry of Jesus, we realize that the spiritual battles He fought with the scribes and Pharisees as well as the priests on the streets by day; He had already won in prayer by night. The Christian of today can glean much by viewing the prayer life of Jesus.

Jesus understood the importance of getting alone with His Father. There were times when He did not want to be around his disciples so he withdrew from them to spend **alone** time with God. As has been stated previously, He did this at different times on different occasions. The important thing for the church to see here is that He prayed. The **Spirit powered church** must pray. Prayer cannot be an afterthought. It must be the lifeline of the church.

Prayer for Others

One of the most interesting aspects of Jesus prayer life was that he spent a lot of time praying for others. Because of this, many came seeking help of various kinds from Jesus. We, in the church, must make time to pray for one another. There are no more powerful words that one can hear than those words, "I'm **praying** for you." The **Holy Spirit** instigates such prayer if we give Him the freedom to do so. However, the Holy Spirit will not **force** Himself upon us. We must **seek** His help and guidance.

Prayer that is fostered by the Holy Spirit of God attracts others. Jesus' disciples came to Him after one of His prayer sessions and said to Him, "... *Lord, teach us to pray,.*" (Luke 11: 1) A praying church will always be a church that naturally births new prayer warriors. That is the plan of God that the Holy Spirit came to implement. We are not talking about making a show of prayer. That is pharisaical and does not please God. Furthermore, the **Holy Spirit** is not a part of that type of prayer. Real prayer does not have to be loud or flamboyant. It does not have to be showy. It must have, however, as its main ingredient the presence and power of the **Holy Spirit**.

Confidence

Jesus' prayer life exhibited real confidence in His Heavenly Father. He knew that His Father always heard Him and would answer His prayer. In many instances, when circumstances seemed humanly impossible, Jesus prayed with confidence and the Father heard and answered. That is the kind of prayer life the **Spirit powered church** must practice. There must be a confidence in the Father when the church prays in order for Him to hear and answer (John 11:42). This **confidence** can be realized in the person of the **Holy Spirit**. The church is taught in the Scripture that it should always pray in Jesus' name. Prayers prayed in Jesus' name will never be overlooked by our Heavenly Father (John 14:13; 15:7; 16:23).

Further, Jesus' prayer life exhibited an absolute obedience to the **will of His Father**. After He prayed and the Father had spoken, He acted upon the Word of God. If the church has any lesson to learn it is this; once we have prayed and heard from God we should be busy doing what He has revealed to us. A prayer life that is a result of the indwelling Holy Spirit will always demand **quick** and **total** obedience. This type of praying always involves the seeking and finding of God's will, not our own.

Why Did Jesus Pray

Being the Son of God, why did Jesus need to pray? Jesus prayed because when He "*… became flesh and dwelt among us…*" (John 1:14) He accepted all the **limitations** of **man.** He was even tempted in all ways just as an ordinary man but without sin (Hebrews 4: 15). He cried (John 4: 6). He wept (John 11:35). He was sometimes troubled (John 12:27). Yet, He was not less than God. Jesus was not born with all the wisdom and knowledge He possessed when He began His public ministry. Yes, He was a very exceptional child. After He was found listening to and questioning the doctors and lawyers in the temple who were astonished by Him, He went back to Nazareth where He **grew in wisdom** and in **stature** and in **favor** with **God** and **man** (Luke 2: 51-52). He demonstrated to us the kind of relationship we can have with God through prayer. He was the God/Man to be sure, but He was man. That is the reason He prayed (See Philippians 2:5-11).

Last Prayers

Of course, some of the most touching poignant prayers of our Savior that we have were the last prayers He prayed at the end of His ministry. There was that long season of prayer in Gethsemane where He prayed about the "cup". His prayer was, "*… O My Father, If this cup cannot pass away from Me unless I drink it, **Your will be done**.*" *(*Matthew 26:42*)* Again, after finding His disciples asleep He asked them *to* "***Watch and pray,** lest you enter into temptation. The **spirit indeed** is willing, but the flesh is weak.*" (Matthew 26:41) Sadly enough, Peter did enter into temptation to the point that he denied the Lord (Matthew 26: 69-72). He ended the second prayer session with the words, "***Your will be done**.*" Here, in the most crucial moment of His earthly life, Jesus submitted Himself to the will of the Father, even as He prayed. What a lesson for us! Our prayers must **always** be subjected to the **will** of the **Father.** The last thing that Jesus did in Gethsemane was to pray. The first thing that He did on the cross was to pray. His desire to avoid the cup was not because of any fear of death. It was not because of the fear of physical pain. It was not the fear of shame. It was the **burden** resting upon Him as the **substitute for our sins** that was the content of the "cup".

On the Cross

On the cross Jesus prayed, *"Father, forgive them, for they do not know what they do." (*Luke 23: 34) This was the final earthly pronouncement of His love for all. It was explicit because no names were mentioned. It was unique because it is answered every day and yet every day some are excluded because they exclude themselves. If anyone ever deserved to pray for Himself, it was Jesus. Yet, He prayed for others. When He cried out *"… My God, My God, why have You forsaken me?"* (Matthew 27: 46) it tells us much. There has never been a cry to God that was so full of anguish. There was an actual, real desertion on the part of God. If anyone should ever be aware and sensitive to the presence of God in His life, it was Jesus, His Son. He had lived His life on the earth in constant communion with God. He had known fellowship with God from the **beginning** as we read about in John 17. God had never failed to answer Him before, but in this moment, God dried up the stream of communion, which had been a ceaseless flow into the life of Jesus. What do we learn? We learn that on Calvary **Jesus bore our Hell**. It is a place of God forsakenness. Whatever else Hell is (Luke 16), it is to be completely cut off from fellowship with God. It does not tell us that God had ceased to be a part of Calvary or that Jesus had ceased to trust the Father. The question was, *"Why?"* The pronoun of address was *"My."* It was in that moment that God *"… made Him who **knew no sin** to be sin for us, that we might become the righteousness of God in Him." (*II Corinthians 5: 21) In that moment He bore all the *"curse"* of sin for us (Galatians 3: 13). It was a scene that a Holy God could not look upon. God placed an accent on the scene when total **darkness** fell upon the earth at mid-day, the earth quaked, graves were opened, and saints came out of them and appeared to many in Jerusalem after the resurrection. **We must understand what happened in that moment!** (Matthew 27: 46-53; Psalm 22:1) As life slipped from His body, Jesus cried, *"it is finished."* There was never a deathbed prayer like this. It means that Jesus had accomplished the sacrificial purpose for which He had come into the world. Our salvation had been purchased with His blood. This tells us that Jesus' life was not taken from Him in some untimely way. It simply tells us that Jesus had come to the end of His earthly ministry at this time and in this way. The closing prayer on the cross was, *"Father, into thy hands I commend my spirit".* John says, *"He bowed His head."* (John 19:30) He did not drop his head. This was a final reverence and submission to the will of the Father. Matthew said, *"He yielded up His spirit."* This tells us that Jesus was in charge of our **redemption** until the very end of His life on earth. He gave His life when He chose, for whom He chose and to whom He chose!

His Promise to Us

Of course, the great promise of our Lord concerning prayer is found in the Sermon on the Mount, *"ask, and it will be given to you; seek, and you will find; knock, and it will be opened to you."* *(*Matthew 7:7) To be sure, we must always condition our prayers based on the **will of God**. In the Upper Room Jesus issued another great promise when He said, *"and whatever you ask in My name, that I will do, **that the Father may be glorified in the Son.**"* (John 14: 13) We should never pray selfishly. We should always pray that whatever we do will **glorify God**. Those are the kinds of prayers that will get a response from God.

In this book, we are concerned about **Spirit powered Christians** who form a **Spirit powered church**. Let us always remember that when the Spirit fell on the church on the day of Pentecost, the disciples had gathered in the Upper Room for a great prayer meeting. The Bible tells us *"these all continued with **one accord** in **prayer** and **supplication**, with the women, and Mary the mother of Jesus, and with His brothers."* (Acts 1: 14) It was in this kind of setting that the **Holy Spirit** fell upon the early church. A sign from Heaven came that sounded like a mighty rushing wind. Cloven tongues of fire (there is that **light** again) sat upon each of them and they began to speak with other tongues (languages) as the **Spirit** gave them utterance (Acts 2: 2-4). What they were speaking was not gibberish. It was not senseless or incoherent babbling. The Scripture is clear that there were people dwelling at Jerusalem who were devout people out of every nation under heaven. When the people heard them, they marveled because the disciples appeared to be Galileans and they were confounded because *"... everyone heard them speak in his **own language**."* (Acts 2: 6) Then the Scripture, further clarifying what happened, said, *"then they were all amazed and marveled, saying to one another, 'Look, are not all these who speak Galileans? And how is it that we hear, each in our own **language in which we were born?**'"* (Acts 2: 7- 8) These verses, forever, dismiss the idea that what the disciples were speaking on the day of Pentecost were ecstatic utterances. The miracle was that the disciples were speaking in tongues (languages) that they had not studied and the people heard in their own language. It was a miracle of communication so that those people who had gathered from all over the known world would be able to go back and carry the gospel to their own people. We will discuss this further when we talk about spiritual gifts.

Space would not permit an exhaustive discussion of all the **answered prayers** that we read about in the New Testament but every Christian knows that **prayer** is that wonderful, personal **validation** of our faith in Jesus Christ as a person of the triune God. Perhaps one of the greatest needs of Christians in this hour is to recognize answered prayer and to bear testimony to others of how God has answered prayer in our lives. Of course, we all understand that God does not always answer our prayers in the way that we expect Him to but even then, we usually always recognize, in hindsight, that God was wise and correct far beyond anything that we could imagine in the way that He did answer our prayers. So many times, God answers our prayers in ways that are far beyond anything that we could have ever hoped for (Ephesians 3: 20-21). Recognizing the answer to prayer and bearing witness of it is one of the great blessings that come with growing in grace. It is a part of the sanctification process.

The Spirit's Intercession

One of the great ministries of the Holy Spirit is that of making intercession for us in prayer. The word of God teaches us that "... *The Spirit also helps in our weaknesses. For we do not know what we should pray for as we ought, but the Spirit Himself makes intercession for us with* **groanings which cannot be uttered.** *Now He who searches the hearts knows what the mind of the* **Spirit** *is, because He makes intercession for the saints* **according to the will of God.**" (Romans 8: 26-27) These "*groanings which cannot be uttered*" means a deep noise that comes from a hopeless situation. They are the result of not knowing what to pray for or how to pray about a certain thing. This groaning can come from pressure and problems we are facing. It may come because of a special need we may have. The problem is, however, our groaning is not enough. The **Holy Spirit** of God intercedes for us and "fills in the blanks" for us at the throne of God.

The day of Pentecost is one of the most powerful manifestations of the power and presence of the **Holy Spirit** in the life of the church that we find in the Bible. To be sure, some have misunderstood and misinterpreted what happened on the day of Pentecost, but we should never allow those who have distorted the Pentecostal manifestation to keep us from studying the Pentecostal experience nor should it deter any church from the same kind of *"prayer and supplication"* that preceded the coming of the Holy Spirit on that day. Of course, there will never be another **Pentecost** just as there will never be another **Calvary.** The church was birthed on the day of Pentecost and it will never need to be re-birthed because the gates of Hell (or Hades) will never prevail against it (Mathew 16:18). There will never be another Calvary because Christ paid the *"once for all"* sacrifice for our sin (Hebrews 10:10; I Peter 1:18).

A Sure Validation

The church must always remember that no church will ever be fruitful in its ministry without the Holy Spirit's guidance and control. Further, one cannot separate the Holy Spirit from the task of the church. God has intentionally intertwined these two in order to get the gospel to the whole world. The church can never hope to accomplish the task of reaching the world with the gospel without the **Holy Spirit**. The reality is that many churches (87% according to the latest stats) have ignored the leadership and power of the Holy Spirit and have replaced Him with the reckless, faulty knowledge and wisdom of man. This, of course, is the reason a record number of churches are closing their doors every week. Because of the church following the wisdom of man rather than the leadership of the Spirit, **pastors** are walking away from ministry positions in record numbers. Because of the absence of the Holy Spirit in the church young people see the hypocrisy left by this void and they leave the church, often never to be active in church again. On the other hand, there are a few churches that "get it." They understand that the most important thing in the life of the church is the presence of the **Holy Spirit**. Simply put, we cannot be the church without **Him.**

Power for Service

The church carries forth the **work** of Jesus under the power of the **Holy Spirit.** The church is energized and led by the power of the **Spirit** and that enables it to implement the work of Jesus in the world. When we live in the presence and power of the Holy Spirit, we become a representative of the "Most High God" to the world,

To be sure, there can be no **real harmony** in the church without the **Holy Spirit**. Often there are situations that arise in the life of a church that seem almost impossible to fix. The "dynamics of disunity" in the church are often complicated but it is safe to say that much of the disunity could be avoided if the church would simply allow the **Holy Spirit** to control its ministry.

Often leaders, deacons, elders, etc. do not handle disunity in the fellowship under the leadership of the Spirit. A group of deacons, after several secret meetings without the pastor, called him in and "fired him." His 12-year-old son and his precious wife were devastated. When Sunday morning arrived, he had nowhere to preach. His family felt violated and abused. As a result, his son does not attend church. Because of an inadequate dismissal package, his financial future was threatened. The deacons admitted there was no real reason for the dismissal other than, in their words, "You're just not taking the church in the direction we want it to go." The devastation the pastor and his family experienced did not matter to those deacons. They did not care about the scars that would be left by their selfish action. Where was the presence of the **Holy Spirit** in this matter? Would the Holy Spirit ever lead a group of men to do such a thing? There is no way the **Holy Spirit** would ever be involved in such a thing. In fact, those kinds of actions anger God and those deacons will give an account of their actions one day.

Disunity

Another church experienced a similar problem and disunity began to divide the congregation. It escalated to the point that a faction in the membership wanted to ask the pastor to resign. The deacons refused to ask for his resignation because they knew he had done nothing that would demand his resignation. They stood with the pastor even though they knew it was a losing battle. The problem got bigger and the pastor decided to resign rather than split the church. The deacons made sure that he was taken care of financially until he could locate another position. That, dear friend, is a validation of the presence of the Holy Spirit in those deacons' lives. The **Holy Spirit** will always lead the church to do the **right thing**.

It is clear that without the **Holy Spirit** the church becomes a purveyor of just another religion because without the Spirit there is no fellowship, no promise, no joy, and no peace. Church becomes mere religious misery. However, when the **Holy Spirit** is given free rein in the church the gospel will be proclaimed, souls will be saved and Jesus will be exalted. The church must always remember that the **Holy Spirit** always works at the behest of Jesus Himself who declared that " ... *when He, the Spirit of truth;*

*has come, He will guide you into all truth; for **He will not speak on His own authority**, but whatever He hears He will speak; and He will tell you things to come. He will glorify Me, for **He will take of what is Mine** and declare it to you. **All things that the Father has are Mine**. Therefore I said that He will take of Mine and declare it to you."* (John 16: 13-15)

It's a Living Organism

The church is a **living organism** and not a mere organization. The **Holy Spirit** makes it so. The Holy Spirit causes us to be a part of a "body" and not a social club. We are called by the Holy Spirit to be participants and not spectators in this organism. The Holy Spirit will cause this "organism" to have people as its primary concern and not programs or buildings. The Holy Spirit helps the church understand that its' most important resources are the Word of God and **prayer**, not human ingenuity or available funds. Do we ever wonder what God would do in the average church if there were a total dependence upon Him to accomplish the work, supply funds and bear fruit for the kingdom and the King's glory?

When the Christian reviews the **Scriptural** validation, the **cosmological** validation, and the validation of our faith through answered **prayer**: he should feel quite secure in faith and should be able to bear daily testimony concerning his faith.

POINTS FOR DISCUSSION

1. "A **Spirit** powered people must have an unshakable assurance of their Biblical faith if they are to have a **Spirit powered church.**" Read I Corinthians 2:14 and discuss it in light of this statement.

2. "The church that would be **Spirit powered** must maintain an unwavering insistence on a regenerate membership." Do you agree with this statement? Why or why not?

3. Because of our permissive society, many young adults simply do not understand the difference between right and wrong. They have no problem with consuming alcohol. They excuse themselves by declaring: "Jesus drank wine (which was not fermented and nothing more than grape juice) so there is nothing wrong with taking a drink now and then." This makes it clear that they have a **disconnect with the Holy Spirit.** Discuss what happens in the believers life when a disconnect between the Holy Spirit and the believer occurs.

4. Carnality was a serious problem in the Corinthian church. Paul said he could not speak to the church because they were no longer spiritual but carnal in every way. It simply means that the **Holy Spirit** was no longer in control. Paul referred to them as "*babes in Christ*" (I Corinthians 3: 1-4 NKJV). How do you think carnality affects the Christian life. How do you think it affects the church?

5. Many Christians have witnessed revival and renewal in the church as the result of the people freely depending on the power of the **Holy Spirit** and allowing Him in His power to validate their faith. In fact, revival comes no other way! Discuss how the church can experience renewal and what role the Holy Spirit has in the renewal process.

6. Prayer is the most personal and indispensable validation of our faith through the ministry of the **Holy Spirit** in our lives. Jesus made it clear for time and eternity that the **Holy Spirit** is ours for the **asking.** What role does the Holy Spirit play in your prayer life?

7. A church experienced a problem and disunity began to divide the congregation. It escalated to the point that a faction in the membership wanted to ask the pastor to resign. The deacons refused to ask for his resignation because they knew he had done nothing that would demand his resignation. They stood with the pastor even though they knew it was a losing battle. The problem got bigger and the pastor decided to resign rather than split the church. The deacons made sure that he was taken care of financially until he could locate another position. That, dear friend, is a validation of the presence of the Holy Spirit in those deacons' lives. The **Holy Spirit** will always lead the church to do the **right thing**. Do you agree or disagree with this?

Step Three
Receive the Empowerment of the Holy Spirit

While the Scripture doesn't give detailed instructions as to how we are to receive the **Holy Spirit**, the most instructive examples in Scripture involve unity, waiting, prayer and supplication (Acts 1: 14). In Luke's moving description of Jesus' ascension scene, and after Jesus had given them a command to be His witnesses, Jesus assured them that He would, *"... send the Promise of My Father upon you; but tarry in the city of Jerusalem until you are endued with **power** from on **high.**"* (Luke 24: 49) This promise, that Peter reminded the people about on the day of Pentecost (Acts 2: 17), is a reference to Joel 2: 28 in which God says, *"... I will pour out **My Spirit** on all flesh..."* It means that there will be no discrimination. The **Spirit** will be available to people of all kindred and nations. It will be available to the young and the old, to men and women, to people of all classes and stations in life. No one will be restricted and no one will be excluded. Anyone who desires the **Spirit** can receive Him. Thus, Jesus declares for time and eternity, the absolute **necessity** and **centrality** of the **Holy Spirit** in carrying out His mission on earth. The mission of the Holy Spirit precedes the mission of the church. It is important that the church have a correct and strong theology of the Holy Spirit. If the Holy Spirit is absent from the church, any type of Christian discipleship is inconceivable. The Holy Spirit is the lifeline of the church. He is the life-giver. He is the personification of truth for the church. He is the unifier in the church. He is the one who brings forth fruit in the life of the church. Without His **power,** there can be no effective witness.

When He gave the command to *"tarry in the city of Jerusalem, **until** you are endued with power from on high,"* the Luke passage was inexorably coupled with the first two chapters of the book of Acts. Our Heavenly Father's desire is for us to be filled with the Holy Spirit's power and be used for Kingdom work. Gasoline is a perfect analogy of power being unleashed. Its power can be seen in at least two ways. Put into a container and ignited gasoline will create the power of an explosion. But, put into the gas tank of an automobile the power is harnessed by the engine. The church cannot be successful with a "flash in the pan" kind of ministry. It must have the presence and power of the Holy Spirit to succeed. It is a spiritual and theological fact that the church will never accomplish great things for the kingdom's sake unless it begins to understand that it must rely solely on the presence and power of the **Holy Spirit** for its lasting power.

Luke opens the Book of Acts by addressing Theophilus, who many believe to have been an official of government, informing him that his "*former treatise*", which was a reference to the Gospel of Luke, was a book which revealed "*all that Jesus **began** both to do and to teach.*" The book of Acts tells what Jesus **continued** to do through **Spirit** filled people. In Acts 1: 3, we have the only reference in the New Testament as to how long Jesus ministered on earth after His resurrection. It was for 40 days. During that period, Jesus established three critical truths related to the mission of the church.

First, He "*... also presented Himself **alive** after suffering by many infallible proofs.*" (Acts 1:3) There must be absolutely no doubt that Jesus has arisen from the grave and conquered sin, death and hell. There were at least 11 appearances of Christ after His resurrection that were recorded in the Scripture. The apostle Paul enumerates some of His appearances and stated that He was seen "*... by over five hundred brethren at once.*" (I Corinthians 15: 6) His final appearance was to the apostle Paul on the Damascus Road (Acts 9: 4, 17). When Jesus made that final appearance to an earthly being, the light of the Lord blinded Saul so that he could not see for 3 days. Saul later received an infilling of the **Holy Spirit** through the ministry of Ananias at the home of Judas on the street called Straight. The **infallible** proofs refer to **indisputable** proofs. It is beyond any reasonable doubt that Jesus arose from the grave. Although Josephus, a highly revered Jewish historian, reported the resurrection of Jesus, we never need to appeal to any outside sources. All the evidence we need is in the Scriptures and there is no empirical or historical evidence to the contrary. **Jesus is alive!** The disciples had to be firmly convinced of His resurrection in order to be effective in their mission. So, likewise, must the church be absolutely convinced that Jesus is alive. If He is alive, and we know that He is, then the church has everything it needs to succeed. The **Holy Spirit** makes Jesus real to the church. Some of the best and most moving worship services held in churches are those Easter services where the church is reminded by the Holy Spirit that Jesus is risen and alive forevermore. Some of the greatest experiences a church can have are in

Easter sunrise services. As the Sun comes up and takes away the darkness, the proclamation of "He is risen" seems to release the power of the Holy Spirit; illuminating the purposes and plans of God for the church. Praise be to God for the resurrection and thanks be to God for the wonderful Holy Spirit who reveals these spiritual truths to us.

Second, Jesus taught them *"of the things pertaining to the kingdom of God ...."* In the Luke passage, Jesus *"... opened their understanding, that they might comprehend the Scriptures. Then He said to them, 'Thus it is written, and thus it was necessary for the Christ to suffer and to rise from the dead the third day, and that repentance and remission of sins should be preached in His name to all nations, beginning at Jerusalem."* (Luke 24: 45 - 47) In Matthew 28, we have an additional word concerning His post-resurrection teachings when He said, *"... All authority has been given to Me in heaven and on earth. Go therefore and make disciples of all nations, baptizing them in the name of the **Father** and of the **Son** and of the **Holy Spirit**, teaching them to **observe all things** that I have commanded you; and lo, I am with you always, even to the end of the age."* (Matthew 28: 18 - 20) Here, we have again the teaching of Jesus concerning His sonship and the **Trinity**. We are to baptize in the name of the **Father**, the **Son**, and the **Holy Spirit**.

After that, we have a teaching responsibility. We are to teach His followers **all** things that He has commanded us. There is never a place for a partial or halfhearted gospel. A **Holy Spirit** powered church will not be an **ordinary** church. Churches, in the absence of the Holy Spirit, become little more that social clubs where well meaning people gather to do their alms before men. They forget that the main mission of the church is to promote the **"good news"**, not the latest **gossip**. Others seem to have drifted into mediocrity and formalism whereby the gospel is preached with little enthusiasm. Sadly enough, this lack of enthusiasm in churches is a sad characteristic of many discouraged congregations. Mediocrity, formalism and lack of enthusiasm, many times results in a lack of acknowledgment and utilization of the Holy Spirit's power. Some are close to death but do not realize the need to change. Still, other churches seem willing to present a compromised gospel. In such cases, there is a void of Holy Spirit power. The Spirit powered church will not be merely social in its approach. Neither will it be mediocre or compromising. Paul warned young Timothy about times like these and that there would be a "form of Godliness but denying its power." (II Timothy 3:5) The church must be **Holy Spirit** motivated to carry the greatest, most wonderful message ever given...**Jesus saves**! We must always declare the **whole counsel** of God and never be ashamed of that message (Romans 1: 16). He has assured us that in that process, He is always with us. How is He with us? He is with us in the person and power of the **Holy Spirit**.

Third, Jesus commanded the early church to tarry in Jerusalem and wait upon the empowerment of the **Holy Spirit**. This is the only thing that will work. Jesus never even hinted that to compromise His doctrine would work. He did not suggest that tolerance of sin in the church would build His church. He built the church in Jerusalem on the rock of **Himself** (Matthew 16:18) in which people who lied to the **Holy Spirit** dropped dead (Acts 5: 1-11). Sometimes Christians get in too much of a rush in doing the work of the Lord. It is as though we sometimes feel that organization, ritual, aesthetic worship or palatial facilities can accomplish the great commission without the **Holy Spirit.** While these things may be nice and helpful, the **Holy Spirit** is the most indispensable ingredient in empowering a church.

In Zechariah 4:6 God spoke to Zechariah concerning the restoration and the renewal of the temple worship. He said it would be accomplished, "... *not by might, nor by power, but by My Spirit...*" It is as though God said to His servant, "I'm going to do a great work but it will be by my **Spirit** and nothing man can conjure up." The Holy Spirit is the most important aspect of the church's power and calling.

Some have compared the average church and how it functions to "rearranging the deck chairs on the Titanic." It does not matter how many new techniques, organizational changes or structural changes are made in the church; it will never be the church that Jesus built until it begins to operate under a greater power than any human can muster. That power can only come from the **Holy Spirit**.

A story is told about a group of bush missionaries that camped near a colony of monkeys for several days. The missionaries recognized that the monkeys seemed to be watching every move they made. The missionaries left for another area to minister. Upon returning to the old campsite they found the colony of monkeys gathering and arranging sticks into a pile that resembled the firewood the missionaries had used. The monkeys all sat around the pile of sticks as if they were sitting around a campfire warming themselves. The only problem was that there was no fire. Sadly enough, some churches operate that way. It has the structure, the programs, the music, and the preaching (all the sticks), but it lacks the fire. The fire, of course, is the **Holy Spirit** and He **desires** to empower the church.

An old man lived near the church in his community. He never attended church, but he was often invited by his neighbors to visit the church. One evening the church building caught fire. The fire trucks from the surrounding areas came to help put out the fire. The old gentleman went to the scene and watched the church building burn. One of the members saw him and sarcastically asked, "Why are you here? You've never cared to come any other time." The old gentleman responded: "The church has never been on fire before!" Maybe, just maybe, some people do not come to our churches because they have never seen any fire there.

It was on the evening of the resurrection day when the disciples were gathered together with the doors shut because they feared the Jews. On this occasion, we have two records of evidence that make the resurrection of Jesus an infallible truth. **First,** Jesus appeared in their midst even though the doors were shut. How could this be? We are talking about a part of the Godhead who created everything. There was a characteristic of His resurrection body that enabled Him to pass through closed doors. We do not understand all about it but that is as **infallible** as it gets! (See I John 3: 2) Moreover, He showed them *"His hands and His side."* The Disciples were gladdened by that experience. **Second**, it is to that group of fearful disciples that Jesus said: *"Peace to you! As the Father has sent Me, I also send you."* At that time He gave them a little foretaste of Pentecost which was ahead when He *"… breathed on them, and said to them, 'Receive the **Holy Spirit**.'"* (John 20: 20-22) How much more powerful could it get! It should be noted that this was the first action of Jesus toward His disciples after His resurrection, which should tell us something of the importance of the **Holy Spirit** in the work of the Lord in the spread of the gospel after His **resurrection** and **ascension**.

Pentecost

After the ascension of Jesus, the disciples of Jesus tarried for 10 days *"with **one accord** in prayer and supplication."* (Acts 1:14). At the end of 10 days was the Feast of Pentecost. The word "Pentecost" simply means "fiftieth." It took place fifty days after the Passover. The feast was a very popular feast because it was a celebration of the completion of grain harvest as well as celebration of the receiving of the law by Moses on Sinai. It was sometimes known as the "Feast of Weeks" (Exodus 34: 22; Deuteronomy 16: 10). It was referred to in Exodus 23: 16 as the "Feast of Harvest." All males were expected to attend this feast. This accounts for the fact that there were "*devout men, out of every nation under heaven*" who were present. Many different languages were represented there. This is the circumstance that prompted the need for the miracle of translation when the disciples began to speak to the people. The people understood in their **own native tongue.** People in such situations tend to gather in language groups. It is apparent that the disciples went to speak to those various language groups and the language groups could hear the disciples in their own **native language.** It was a miraculous Divine plan on the day of Pentecost that would send the gospel message to all parts of the world. This ministry happened because the "*Spirit gave them utterance.*" There was the **sound** of a mighty rushing wind and the **appearance** of tongues of fire. This was a manifestation of the power of the **Spirit. Wind** and **fire** appear in the Old Testament as signs of the **presence** of **God.** When God delivered the Philistines into the hands of David, He commanded David to go around them and wait at the mulberry trees until he should hear " *...the sound of marching in the tops of the mulberry trees.*" and that is when he should attack (II Samuel 5: 24). In Psalm 104: 3, the mighty God is described as one "*... who walks on the wings of the wind.*" As has been mentioned earlier, the Lord appeared to Moses as a flame of fire that did not consume the burning bush. That is the reason that Moses turned aside to investigate. When he drew near the burning bush God commanded him to remove his shoes for he was standing on holy ground in the **presence** of the Lord (Exodus 3: 2-5). When the Israelites left Egypt, God guided them with a cloud by day and pillar of **fire** by night. These guides were not taken away (Exodus 13: 21-22). The cloud and the pillar of fire are two great symbols suggesting to us the irresistible nature of the **Spirit's** power.

Prophecy Fulfilled

Peter recognized that the disciples were "*all filled with the **Holy Spirit**"* and that this was a fulfillment of **Joel's prophecy** recorded in Joel 2: 28. Some who heard them were amazed and were asking "*... whatever could this mean? (Acts 2: 12)* Some mocked them. The word that is translated "*mocking*" literally means "*to joke*" (Verse 13). Peter recognized the seriousness of mocking the **Holy Spirit.** Apparently, some accused them of being drunk. That is when Peter stood up and began to preach his famous sermon on that day of Pentecost. Some scholars suggest that Peter preached for about 12 minutes. This is not to suggest that all sermons are to be brief, because the Apostle Paul was sometimes "long" in preaching (Acts 20:10). The Jews who gathered there were **devout** Jews and they would immediately recognize the prophecy of Joel. In the face of this overwhelming and irresistible demonstration of the **Spirit's** power, the people were "*...cut to the heart,*" (Acts 2:37) and asked Peter and the rest of the apostles: *"What shall we do?"* Peter called upon them to repent. Repentance is a Christian absolute. It means to "change the mind" about God, Jesus Christ and sin! Jesus made that clear in Luke 13: 3. Believers were called upon to be baptized as a sign of *"the remission of sins"* (verse 38). As a result, they would receive the gift of the **Holy Spirit.** This was a part of the apostolic proclamation (katangello-**καταηγγέλλω**). This verse should never be distorted in any teaching that baptism is necessary to salvation. Baptism is a matter of obedience and testimony (see Romans 6: 3-5). At the house of Cornelius, the **Holy Spirit** fell upon the hearers of Peter's sermon **before** they were baptized (Acts 10: 44 - 47). We must always be careful that our teachings are consistent with the teachings of the Scriptures. **This power came to the disciples because they waited and "continued with one accord in prayer and supplication."** (Acts 1: 14)

We all receive the Holy Spirit when we are saved (I Corinthians 12: 13). The "indwelling" of the Holy Spirit refers to that salvation. George Whitfield said that the indwelling of the Spirit is "the common privilege of all believers." There is a vast difference between "indwelling" and "infilling." It is the Holy Spirit who convicts us of our sin and our need for salvation. As a result of that conviction, we are brought to a point of regeneration. We are saved! Then the Holy Spirit takes up residence in our lives and, as a result, seals us for eternity. In the book of Acts, Jesus instructed the disciples to remain in Jerusalem and wait for the Holy Spirit's power to come upon them (Acts 1:4). It must be understood that the Holy Spirit is not an option in the Christian's life. It is clear that without the Holy Spirit there is no salvation (Romans 8:9). The last part of verse 9 says "... *now if anyone does not have the **Spirit** of Christ, he is not His."*

The Holy Spirit not only convicts us but we receive Him upon our acceptance of Jesus Christ as our Savior and thereafter and always, He is available to us. As pointed out previously, this is not something that is a kind of "second blessing" but something that equips us for service. It was the announcement of John the Baptist that Jesus would baptize with the Holy Spirit (John 1: 33). This happened to Jesus at the beginning of His public ministry. After His baptism, the Holy Spirit descended upon Him like a dove and later led Him into the wilderness where He was tempted of the devil for forty days after which He began His Galilean ministry. It was at His baptism that John recognized Him as the *"Lamb of God"* (verse 36). The baptism of the Holy Spirit is a special experience in which the Christian receives all of the Holy Spirit that he can possibly contain. It carries with it the connotation of the impartation of the very power of God into the life of the believer. The term suggests an abundant supply. It was a fulfilling, authenticating experience in the life of the disciples on the day of Pentecost. It was from there that they went out into the world to turn the world upside down (Acts 17:6). After Jesus informed the disciples that they would be baptized with the Holy Spirit *"... not many days from now."* (Acts 1: 5), they were to be witnesses to all the peoples of the world. While they would begin at Jerusalem and then to Judea and later to Samaria, they would also carry the gospel to *"... the end of the earth."* (Acts 1: 8) While there is one baptism of the Spirit, there are many infillings of the Spirit. It was Peter's promise to the multitudes gathered at Jerusalem that if they would repent of their sins and be baptized in the name of Jesus Christ that they would *"... receive the gift of the Holy Spirit."* (Acts 2: 38) So, the disciples who had received the Holy Spirit in the upper room (John 20:20) received an even greater infilling on the day of Pentecost.

Lame Man

After Peter and John had healed the lame man (Acts 3: 6), they went on to Solomon's Porch where the lame man, who had been healed, held Peter and John and a multitude gathered about them. Peter assured them that it was not by his or John's personal power that the man was made whole. It was by the resurrected Christ and faith in His name that this man was made whole. Peter called upon them to repent and be converted so that their sin could be blotted out. When Peter and John were hauled before Annas and his kindred, Peter *"... filled with the Holy Spirit,"* (Acts 4: 8) assured them that the man was made whole by the resurrected Christ. Again, we witness this "power" (dunamis-δύναμις) of heaven and earth which had been given to Jesus, being given unto the apostles as promised (Matthew 28:18; Luke 24: 49; Acts 1:8). Peter also asserted that there was *"no other name under heaven given among men by which we must be saved."* (Acts 4: 12)

In Acts 8: 14 - 17 Peter and John went to Samaria where the people had received the Word of God and **prayed** for the new Christians that they *"might receive the* **Holy Spirit."** Note how often the **Holy Spirit** responds to **prayer.** In Acts 28: 25, we have a record of the **Holy Spirit speaking through the Scriptures.** There are a number of references in the Scripture in which the **Spirit** spoke to the disciples such as we have in Acts 10: 19 when Peter was at the house of Simon the Tanner. When the Jewish Christians contended with Peter about speaking to the gentiles Peter stated to them that "*the Spirit told me to go with them, doubting nothing.*" (Acts 11: 12) We see on this occasion and many other occasions that the **Spirit** directed the disciples to ministry such as we find in Acts 13: 4 where the **Holy Spirit** sent Paul and Barnabas to Cyprus.

Infillings

The **Holy Spirit** not only empowers the believer for service but also gives direction. There are **many infillings** of the Holy Spirit in the life of the believer. What does the "infilling" of the Holy Spirit really mean? The concept of "infilling" refers to control. When we are filled with the Holy Spirit, we come under the absolute control of the Holy Spirit. The Christian who allows the Holy Spirit to use them will accomplish the will and work of the living God.

It should be said at this point that many Christians shy away from the Holy Spirit and His power because they are uncomfortable with this "infilling." Some equate this with such things as miraculous powers to heal, speaking in unknown tongues or being "slain" in the Spirit. Any scholar of the word of God knows well that the infilling does not refer to such activities but rather to a Spirit controlled life that depicts Jesus in us regularly and consistently.

Ephesians 5:18 says, "*and do not be drunk with wine, in which is dissipation; but be **filled with the Spirit**.*" In this passage, Paul is drawing an analogy between intoxication by alcohol and control by the Holy Spirit. To be "filled' with wine does not mean that you are filled completely. It means that the alcohol affects every part of the body. A person's walk, speech, thoughts, sight and hearing are all affected by alcohol in the body. When one is "filled" with the Spirit, it profoundly means that every action is brought under His control. The infilling of the Holy Spirit literally means that He takes absolute control of our lives. **He possesses us!** It is also true that if the Spirit possess us, Satan cannot.

D. L. Moody, while speaking to a large audience, held up an empty glass and asked the question, "How can I get the air out of this glass?" One man from the back of the room shouted, "Suck it out with a pump!"

Moody replied, "That would create a vacuum and shatter the glass." Many other suggestions came from the crowd then Moody picked up the glass and then a pitcher of water and began to pour water into the glass. When he had filled the glass to the top he said, "There, all the air is now removed." Then he explained that victory in the Christian life is not acquired by human methods but by "*being filled with the Holy Spirit.*"

How We Receive Him

It is the **Holy Spirit** who constantly infills us and directs us in our service to the Lord, Jesus Christ! The only instruction as to how we receive Him is found in the Scriptures that tell us of the disciples waiting at Jerusalem where they engaged in "***prayer and supplication.***" They were also in "***one accord.***" When this happens in the life of a church, that church becomes a **Spirit powered church.** The Holy Spirit is **ours for the asking** (Luke 11:13). However, Jesus laid down a very indispensable principle in the fact that we must **ask believing** (Matthew 21:22)!

We see, moreover, that the **Spirit powered church** is a church that can accept needed change. The brethren at the church in Jerusalem contended with Peter because he preached to the gentiles at the house of Cornelius (Acts 10: 34-40). Peter recited to them what the **Holy Spirit** had led him to do and the matter is closed in Acts 11: 18 telling us, "*When they heard these things they became silent; and they glorified God, saying, 'Then God has also granted to the Gentiles repentance.'*" This caused the brethren at Jerusalem to change their tradition of speaking only to the "circumcision" and **opened their eyes** to the purpose of God in reaching out to all the peoples of the earth. It was then that they understood the Lord's commission in Acts 1: 8 and the need to carry the gospel to the "*end of the earth.*" The **Spirit powered church** will not hang on to customs and traditions that do not serve the **Spirit** of God in this day. They can accept needed change as the brethren of Jerusalem did.

The **Holy Spirit** also **reveals** God's purpose in the life of the **Spirit powered church** and leads believers to look outside themselves for God's purpose. It is that same **Spirit** that **inspires** the **Spirit powered church** to undertake great things for God. In fact, in Paul's letter to the Ephesians we have the command to abstain from all kinds of ungodly behavior. We are to "*walk circumspectly, not as fools but as wise.*" (Ephesians 5: 15) The term "walk" refers to the **way we live our lives!** It is capped with the admonition of Ephesians 5: 18, which we have already discussed.

Results

There were some earth shaking results of the baptism of the **Holy Spirit** upon those early disciples on the day of Pentecost and any church that wants to be a **Spirit powered church** will have to demonstrate to the world that they indeed **are** made up of a **Spirit** filled people.

First, the filling of the **Spirit** turned those early disciples into evangelists. After Peter preached, and the people posed the question: "*What shall we do?*"; Peter called upon them to repent and be baptized in the name of Jesus Christ which would result in the remission of sins and the gift of the **Holy Spirit** (Acts 2: 38). Peter then gave an invitation. A church that does not give an invitation is a church that will never grow.

There are some pastors who believe that no invitation should be given in the church. They say, "If God wants to save them He will. It's not our business." This is bordering on heresy. God expects people who have heard the gospel to be given an opportunity to respond. A young evangelist was preaching an evangelistic meeting in a church when the pastor of the church quenched the Spirit. The young evangelist had preached a great gospel message with conviction and was giving the invitation. Many people stood in the aisle to receive Christ as their savior. After a few minutes, the pastor of the church stopped the music and discontinued the invitation. Many people who were in the aisle on the way to make life-changing decisions were sent back to their seats and the invitation was concluded. The evangelist was surprised. After the service, the evangelist asked the pastor, "Why did you stop the invitation? Those people were responding to receive Christ." The pastor replied, "They don't need the invitation to get saved." That church never grew under that pastor's leadership.

The Bible says plainly of Peter that "*... with many other words he testified and exhorted them, saying, 'Be saved from this perverse generation.'*" (Acts 2: 40) This passage does not mean that baptism is essential to salvation. It is, however, essential to **obedience**. It is part of the great commission of Matthew 28, which tells us that we are to teach all nations and baptize them in the name of the **Father**, the **Son** and the **Holy Spirit**. Baptism must be believer's baptism. Only those "*... who gladly received his word were baptized.*" (Acts 2: 41) Baptism was a door to the church. After baptism that day, about 3,000 souls were added to the church. Romans 6 makes it clear that only believers must be baptized and that baptism is a testimony of our belief in the death, burial and resurrection of Jesus Christ and what Christ has done in the believer's life. It is an individual testimony that every Christian is to bear. This was the thrust of Evangelism Explosion, one of the greatest evangelism tools available to the local church. The late Dr. D. James Kennedy spent his life perfecting that program and God has used it successfully across denominational lines. The heart of Evangelism Explosion is the multiplication of witnesses. Every person trained in EE is expected to become a trainer and in turn enlist two more people to train. Many EE trainers attest to the fact that the most difficult part of the program is enlisting trainees. The primary excuse that is given is, "I really don't have the ability to be involved in this program." People are naturally afraid of sharing their faith but the church needs to know that the **Holy Spirit** is in the business of turning spiritual weaklings into **dynamic witnesses**.

A perfect example is seen in the weakness of that rag tag group of Jesus' disciples. For all practical purposes, most of these men were spiritual weaklings. Peter, when threatened, lied about knowing Jesus. Thomas doubted Jesus' authenticity. Most of them deserted Him in times of real need. Isn't it amazing that Jesus still used them to carry out His plan? The Scripture says that they *"turned the world upside down."* (Acts 17:6) If God could use this group of liars, wimps and deserters, how much more can He use the church today to change the world with the gospel? They became witnesses, not because of their abilities or good traits, but because they were empowered by the **Holy Spirit**.

Second, the **Holy Spirit** produced a hunger and a thirst to know more about Christ and the Christian life. It is an affirmation of Jesus when He cried: *"If any one **thirsts**, let him come to Me and drink. He who believes in Me, as the **Scripture** has said, out of his heart will flow rivers of living water. But this He spoke concerning the **Spirit,** whom those believing in Him would **receive**; for the **Holy Spirit** was not yet given, because Jesus was not yet glorified."* (John 7:34-38) This represented a libation (poured water) of the **Holy Spirit**! A wonderful contemporary Christian song says, "Lord, I want to know you more." This is the cry of too few souls in the church. A pastor once told of a very elderly church member that everyone called Aunt Mamie. Aunt Mamie was a wonderful Christian who loved her Lord, her church and her pastor. She had real difficulty seeing clearly but that never caused her to slow down. The pastor visited Aunt Mamie weekly because she was such a blessing to him. She would tell her pastor, at the end of each visit, of her love and support for him. Then they would pray. As they knelt in the kitchen of that old farmhouse, Aunt Mamie would begin to pray and the power of the Holy Spirit would fill the room. Her fervent prayer was "Lord I want to know you better!" What a beautiful picture of what the **Holy Spirit** had done in this faithful lady's life. He desires to do this same thing for every believer; if He is allowed to do so. She was Godly but never satisfied with her walk. She always wanted more. The presence of the Holy Spirit will always make us want to know Christ more. He will make us thirst after Christ! A sure sign that the Holy Spirit is active in your life is a genuine desire to know and obey the Savior. If that desire is not present, maybe the Holy Spirit is not present!

A Holy Thirst

Is your church **thirsty?** The emphasis of the early church was not getting out at noon but how much they could learn about what God would have them do. This writer once heard an old evangelist express regret that many Churches begin at eleven o'clock sharp and closed at twelve o'clock dull. The Christians who were saved on the day of Pentecost *"continued steadfastly in the apostles' doctrine and fellowship, in the breaking of bread, and in prayers."* (Acts 2:42) This says something to churches who do not want to emphasize doctrine. A church that does not emphasize the doctrine of the New Testament will be a shallow and ill-informed church that can hardly operate in the power of the **Spirit.** The power of the **Spirit** and sincere belief in **Biblical doctrine** go hand in hand. This writer once heard the testimony of a pastor who was greeting people at the door. He often preached on doctrinal themes. A lady, who thought she was sophisticated, came by and said, *"I enjoyed the sermon today, it didn't have no doctrine nor **nothing**."* The pastor was insulted because he felt that she was being critical of his practice of preaching on doctrinal themes. A pastor should never let his pulpit ministry be guided by people who are shallow and want everyone else to be shallow. It may be well to address contemporary issues in the pulpit but such messages must always be couched in the framework of **New Testament doctrine** because it is quite impossible to preach the gospel of Jesus Christ without teaching **His** doctrine.

A Strong Fellowship

Third, there was a new level of fellowship. There had been periods of broken fellowship even among the disciples. Many times the disciples were concerned about greatness. Once they came to Jesus asking, *"...Who* *then is greatest in the kingdom of heaven?"* (Matthew 18:1) Even as Jesus was making His final journey to Jerusalem where He would be crucified, the Mother of James and John approached Him and asked, "... *that these two sons of mine may sit, one on Your right hand and the other on the left, in Your kingdom."* (Matthew 20: 21) When the other disciples heard about it, they were *"moved with indignation against the two brothers." (*Matthew 20: 24) Now, since they are filled with the **Holy Spirit**, all of that envy and strife is gone. After Simon Peter had argued with God on the housetop of Simon the Tanner (Acts 10:14), he went to the house of Cornelius where he witnessed Gentiles receiving Christ and being filled with the **Holy Spirit**. When the brethren who were Jewish heard about him preaching to the Gentiles, they *"contended with him."* When the Jewish brethren heard Peter sharing what had happened at the house of Cornelius and on the housetop of Simon the Tanner, "... *they became silent; and they **glorified** God, saying, 'Then God has also granted to the Gentiles repentance to life.'"* (Acts 11:18) These men were staunch, Jewish Christians who held some prejudice against Gentiles but were changed when the **Holy Spirit** filled their lives. They acknowledged that they were wrong and they showed a willingness to do the right thing by Gentiles who had received Christ. In the **Spirit powered church,** the most stubborn, obstinate, contrary and negative people experience a sweetness of fellowship and a willingness to change old, obstructive, ungodly habits when they arc filled with the **Spirit.** They become more interested in doing the work of the living Lord than in upholding old family or church traditions that have nothing to do with the fullness of the **Spirit** and may even hinder the fellowship of the church.

A key factor involved in having a great church fellowship is **dying to self.** There can be no fellowship among believers if they are self-centered and self absorbed. There can be no **dying to self** apart from the **Holy Spirit**. Fellowship is a great work of the Holy Spirit but it can only be experienced when and if the church deals with self. The church cannot be full of itself. It must be full of the Holy Spirit. When there is self centeredness in the church there may be division and strife but no fellowship. The early church knew Godly fellowship because of its relationship with the **Holy Spirit**. They loved one another, encouraged and cared for one another. Their fellowship was so strong that they shared their possessions with one another. Something the church needs to remember is that when there is real fellowship there will be seekers who desire to participate in that fellowship. Real **Holy Spirit** fellowship is a powerful invitation to a lost world, to come and drink from the springs of living water (John 4: 10-14).

For some churches to experience this kind of fellowship there will be a need for real repentance. Sometimes churches have experienced this Holy **Spirit** induced **fellowship until** they took their eyes off Christ the Lord. Then they began to find fault. This happened at Corinth. They had developed a Spirit of partisanship in the church and contentions had ensued. Paul pleaded with them to *"speak the same thing"* and that *"there be no divisions among you."* The house of Chloe had reported contentions among them. Paul calls on them to *"be perfectly joined together in the same mind"* because Christ is not divided (I Corinthians 1: 9 - 13). If the **Holy Spirit** is grieved, there will be a **contrary Spirit**.

One church comes to mind as we discuss this concept. This church had a wonderful fellowship and the church was powerful in its outreach and its fellowship. The pastor made a few mistakes and a few very loud critics noticed the mistakes and made them bigger than they were. The talk multiplied and the spiritual power began to dwindle. The fellowship began to break apart and friendships became strained. Once a great fellowshipping, **Holy Spirit** led church was now bickering and fighting over insignificant matters. It took weeks of prayer, loving and preaching to get the fellowship back to where it should have been. However, it did not come easily. There was a time of great brokenness and repentance but through the process relationships were mended, hearts were healed and the Holy Spirits power was realized once again.

Spirit Power

Fourth, the fullness of the **Spirit** enabled the apostles to do *"many wonders and signs"* (Acts 2: 43) A church can do little unless there is the power of the **Spirit** present. Spirit filled people build great churches. People who care little about the presence of the Holy Spirit often maintain small, stagnant or dying churches.

A church in a large Georgia city is a clear example of stagnation and death. The church declined in membership from 550 in Sunday School to 30. A tragic series of events caused the decline. The process of decline began when a faction of disgruntled people began attacking the pastor. The attacks grew stronger and more volatile and finally the faction left to form another church. This left 300 people in the church. Then the church called an interim pastor who had little experience in dealing with church conflict. As a result, 220 more people left. When the church finally called a pastor the church was averaging 60-70 in attendance. The new pastor had very little pastoral experience and because of his approach to ministry, the church fell to 30 in attendance. As a last resort, the Association was called to help. By this time, the Holy Spirit was nowhere to be found in the church. Even the ones left were bickering among themselves and sporadic in attendance. The small church became stagnant and began to die a slow death.

The Director of Missions in the Association led the church to dissolve and restarted the church under a new name with a Biblical approach. A church planter/pastor was called to begin the church and today the church is doing well. The health of the congregation today is a direct result of the presence and power of the **Holy Spirit**. The Spirit has once again been given His rightful place in the fellowship.

The **Holy Spirit** always brings great vision. The early church took the command of Jesus in Acts 1:8 seriously. Peter had gone to Joppa and Caesarea. Already the disciples were moving out of Jerusalem to other places like Samaria with the gospel of Jesus Christ. It was on the day of Pentecost that the **mission movement was born**. Those people who were gathered there from every nation under the sun carried the gospel back to their own people. That is probably the reason Paul often found Christians already gathering and worshipping in locations he visited during his missionary journeys.

Because the early Christians were severely persecuted, they pooled their resources and *"had all things in common."* (Acts 2: 44) This was something they did voluntarily. It was not a government mandate. It was not recommended as a form of government. The old Communists of the Marxist stripe often quoted this passage of Scripture in support of their ideas, even though they were atheists, but this particular type of communal living was not something that was forced upon people by government decree. These early Christians, who were under persecution, had all things in common as a matter of survival. This is born out in Chapter 5 of Acts. Ananias and Sapphira had apparently made public statements about their intention to sell a possession and give the money to the church. However, they did not do as they promised but they held back part of the price. Ananias' wife was privy to it also. When Ananias came in and laid a part of it at the apostles' feet, Peter was obviously grieved in his heart and said: *"Ananias, why has Satan filled your heart to lie to the **Holy Spirit** and keep back part of the price of the land for yourself? While it* remained, **was it not your own?** *And after it was sold,* **was it not in your own control?** *Why have you conceived this thing in your heart? You have not lied to* **men** *but to* **God**." (Acts 5: 3-4) Peter made it clear to them that they had not been forced to sell the land and they could have done whatever they wanted with the money. Their problem was that they had lied to the **Holy Spirit** because of their selfish greed and said that part was all of their commitment. Christians who are tempted to lie about their commitment or to renege on their commitment that they make to the Lord's Body, which is the church, will do well to remember what happened to Ananias and Sapphira. They both fell dead right there in the church. What a rebuke this is to so many in today's church who seem to think nothing of lying to the **Holy Spirit** and making commitments that they are not willing to keep. How many have gone to an early grave because they have lied to God? It is a **serious matter!**

Boldness

Fifth, the **Holy Spirit** gave these early Christians a boldness that they had never known before. Even in the midst of persecution, they continued to go to the Temple **daily** and to break bread from house to house. They "*did eat their meat with gladness and singleness of heart*" (Acts 2: 46). Did the persecution dampen their spirits? Their spirits were not dampened in the least! They were "*praising God and having favor with all the people. And the Lord added to the church* **daily** *those who were being saved*." (Acts 2: 47)

Peter and John were called on the carpet for their healing of the lame man and their preaching in the temple on Solomon's Porch. Peter, the man who, at one time, warmed himself by the enemy's fire in Caiaphas' Palace and denied the Lord three times in his moment of cowardice, answered them saying: "*Let it be known to you all, and to all the people of Israel, that by the name of Jesus Christ of Nazareth, whom you crucified, whom God raised from the dead, by Him this man stands here before you whole*." (Acts 4:10) What he said was not popular among those who were gathered there but Peter now has a new **courage** and the **Holy Spirit** made the **difference!** He did not shy away from naming the name of Jesus Christ as the cause of the man's healing. He claimed nothing for himself but he did not stop there. He declared that, "*this is the stone which was rejected by you builders, which has become the chief cornerstone*." (Acts 4:11 & Matthew 21:42)

When they saw the **boldness** of Peter and John, *"and seeing the man who had been healed standing with them, they could say **nothing** against it."* (Acts 4:14) When their accusers took counsel among themselves, their conclusion was that a great miracle had occurred and they said, *"We cannot deny it."* When a church manifests **Holy Spirit power,** the world can **say nothing against it** (at least, nothing credible)!

When the Priests threatened them and demanded that they not speak in the name of Jesus anymore, Peter and John's answer was, *"We cannot but speak the things which we have seen and heard."* (Acts 4:20) What was the response of the church when Peter and John revealed to them the threatenings that were directed toward them? They prayed. What did they pray for? They prayed that the Lord would *"...Grant to your servants that with all **boldness** they may speak Your word."* (Acts 4:29) They also wanted power to perform great things in *"... the name of Your holy Servant Jesus."* (Verse 30) What was the answer? The answer was that: *"The place where they were assembled together was shaken; and they were all filled with the **Holy Spirit** and they spoke the word of God with boldness."* (Acts 4: 31) This is another **infilling** of the **Holy Spirit.**

After the incident with Ananias and Sapphira, the apostles were gathered on Solomon's Porch where the people magnified them and believers *"were increasingly added to the Lord, multitudes both of men and women."* (Acts 5:14) Then, they had to deal with the High Priest and his henchmen who were greatly disturbed because they were bringing the sick and laying them in the path that they might be healed when the **shadow** of Simon Peter passed over them. The temple guard laid hands on the apostles and put them in a common prison but an **angel** delivered them during the night. When the guard came the next day to arraign them, they found the prison empty and the apostles were out in the temple preaching in the name of **Jesus** again! It was the name of Jesus that so disturbed the priests and the elders of Jerusalem. They realized that His name had **power.** They felt that they had to do something to stop the preaching in the name of Jesus. They feared the power of that **name!** When they hauled the apostles before the council, and the High Priest asked them saying, *"Did not we strictly command you not to teach in this **name**? And look, you have **filled** Jerusalem with your **doctrine**, and intend to bring this Man's blood on us!"* (Acts 5: 28) What was the answer of Peter and the other apostles? They answered: *"We ought to obey God rather than men."* (Verse 29) What a change in the lives of the men who were cowering in fear after the crucifixion (John 20: 19)! The priests and elders (the council) disposed of the matter by beating the apostles and threatening them again. How did they receive the beating? They *"...departed from the presence of the council, rejoicing that they were counted **worthy** to suffer **shame for His name.**"* What a difference the **Spirit made** (Acts 5:41)! Are we ready to suffer **shame** for **His name** in **times like these?**

Many Christians are intimidated by the world. As a result, there is little or no witness for Christ. The kind of boldness that it takes to speak out when no one else will can only come through the Holy Spirit.

John was troubled for some time with the conviction that God was calling him into the ministry. As he worked every day to provide for his family, the gnawing feeling would not leave. John answered the call of the Holy Spirit with the same old excuse every time conviction came... "I cannot speak in front of people. I am shy and timid. God, you have the wrong person. You should call someone else." John went for one year running from the call of God on his life until one day he gave in and cried out to God... "OK, God if you can use me, I'm yours!" Today, John has a very successful ministry and is reaching many people with the Gospel. The man who at one time said, "I can't do it." now says, "When I followed the leading of the Holy Spirit, I realized that He would empower me with a holy boldness that I had never experienced before." The same boldness that John now experiences every day in his ministry is available to every Christian and to his church. We need His boldness to change the world.

Conclusion

In conclusion, we understand that there are no detailed instructions in the New Testament concerning how we go about receiving the **Holy Spirit** but we do have **examples aplenty.** The disciples waited in Jerusalem to receive the *"promise of the Father"* that was given in Joel 2: 28. They continued in **prayer** and **supplications** for ten days and it was on the day of Pentecost that the **Spirit** fell. It was a fulfillment of Jesus' promise to them that they would *"be baptized with the **Holy Spirit** not many days hence."* They had that **thirst** that Jesus promised would be satisfied with the gift of the **Holy Spirit** (John 7:37 & 38). Dear reader, can you also believe that Jesus keeps His promises? We know that there were no longer divisions among them because they were *"in **one accord.**"* As we have pointed out earlier in this volume, it was the promise of Jesus, Himself that the **Holy Spirit** will be given unto them that *"ask Him."* It is clear that an experience of salvation preceded the baptism of the **Holy Spirit** as we see plainly at the House of Cornelius. We understand that there is a **special baptism** of the **Holy Spirit** but that is not the end of **Holy Spirit** activity in the life of the believers or the church. There are any number of infillings of the **Spirit.** There is no mistake that the **Holy Spirit** changes our attitudes, our lifestyle, our motivation and our depth of commitment. Old tensions among the disciples were dispelled. Old meaningless traditions were cast aside because they were a hindrance to the spread of the gospel as we see following the service at the House of Cornelius, where Gentiles were saved and received the **Spirit** even though they were not of the "circumcision." The **Holy Spirit** brought a new spirit of boldness to the Apostles. Simon Peter who once cowered in fear and finally denied the Lord three times while he was warming by the enemy's fire received a **Holy Boldness**. The disciples who were once hiding behind closed doors after the crucifixion of our Lord now rejoiced after they were beaten for preaching in the name of Christ in Jerusalem because they were counted **worthy** to suffer **shame** for the **name** of Christ. What a change the **Holy Spirit** made in their lives!

What the church needs more than anything is to be aware of the Holy Spirit's manifestation of Himself through His power. The church does not need more theory about the Holy Spirit. It does not need more knowledge of the Holy Spirit. It needs the presence and **power** of the Holy Spirit. Words often mean little. Theory is subjective. Human knowledge cannot fathom the power. The church needs the power of the **Holy Spirit** so the **reality of Jesus Christ** might become real in our world!

It is through the quiet but powerful work of the Holy Spirit that the will of God is made known in our lives. He guides us to the tasks that the Lord has for us. He changes minds and hearts. He quietly heals that sick person that you have prayed for. He gives strength in times of trouble. In times of grief he comes along beside us. A. J. Sims in his hymn, *The Unseen Hand*, says it well: ***"There is an unseen hand to me, That leads thru ways I can not see; While going thru this world of woe, This hand still leads me as I go. I'm trusting to the unseen hand, That guides me thru this weary land; And some sweet day I'll reach that strand, Still guided by the unseen hand."***

POINTS OF DISCUSSION

1. Do you agree with the following statement of the authors, "Jesus declares for time and eternity, the absolute **necessity** and **centrality** of the **Holy Spirit** in carrying out His mission on earth. The mission of the Holy Spirit precedes the mission of the church." Why or why not?

2. Gasoline is a perfect analogy of the power of the Holy Spirit unleashed. Its power can be seen in at least two ways. Put into a container and ignited gasoline will create the power of an explosion. But, put into the gas tank of an automobile the power is harnessed by the engine. The church cannot be successful with a "flash in the pan" kind of ministry. Explain how the church can have REAL POWER to do the work of God!

3. The church must be absolutely convinced that Jesus is alive. If He is alive, and we know that He is, then the church has everything it needs to succeed. The **Holy Spirit** makes Jesus real to the church. Is the Holy Spirit all the church needs to succeed?

4. Jesus commanded the early church to tarry in Jerusalem and wait upon the empowerment of the **Holy Spirit**. Do you wait/tarry on the empowerment of the Holy Spirit in your own life? What do you do to receive that power?

5. It does not matter how many new techniques, organizational changes or structural changes are made in the church; it will never be the church that Jesus built until it begins to operate under a greater power than human power. That power can only come from the **Holy Spirit**. How does the Holy Spirit affect our techniques, organization and various changes in the church?

6. We all receive the Holy Spirit when we are saved (I Corinthians 12: 13). The "indwelling" of the Holy Spirit refers to that salvation. George Whitfield said that the indwelling of the Spirit is "the common privilege of all believers." However, there is a vast difference between "indwelling" and "infilling." There are **many infillings** of the Holy Spirit in the life of the

believer. What does the "infilling" of the Holy Spirit really mean? How is it different from "indwelling?"

7. The **Holy Spirit** also **reveals** God's purpose in the life of the **Spirit powered church** and leads believers to look outside themselves for God's purpose. It is that same **Spirit** that **inspires** the **Spirit powered church** to undertake great things for God. What great things has the Holy Spirit inspired you to do for God recently? Your church?

Step Four
Select Spirit Powered Leadership

The congregation that desires a **Spirit powered church** must begin by seeking out and calling a **Spirit filled pastor**. No congregation will ever rise above the pastor. If the pastor is a Spirit filled man who desires a **Spirit powered church,** it can happen. If the pastor does not have a passion for the development of a Spirit powered church, it can never happen. The process begins with a **pastor search committee.** Unless the committee is made up of Spirit filled people, they are not likely to find and recommend a Spirit filled pastor. If they do find such a pastor it will usually be by accident. The congregation that desires to be a **Spirit powered church** must be sure that the search committee is seeking such a person. That means that care must be exercised in selection of the search committee. In some churches the search committee is recommended by the deacon body. In others, the committee is recommended by a nominating committee. No one should be placed on the committee simply because they are wealthy. No one should be placed on the committee simply because they come from the "right family". No one should serve on the committee simply because they have "influence".

Why is it so important that the pastor search committee and the pastor be Spirit filled? The answer is obvious; a **Spirit filled** pastor search committee will always search for a Spirit filled pastor. Being Spirit filled insures a greater effectiveness as servants of the Lord in the church. A search committee that has someone that is not Spirit filled on it will likely have a problem calling a Spirit filled pastor. People who do not walk in the power of the Holy Spirit will usually make decisions based on knowledge, abilities or intellect. Decisions about calling a Spirit filled pastor made with human intellect will always be faulty. For the church to be Spirit powered it must be led by a man of God who is **Spirit powered**. Herein lies the problem in many churches that are floundering because they have leadership in place who were not chosen and placed there by the Holy Spirit. As a result, the church is not being led by the Holy Spirit. It is sad to see so many evangelical and traditional churches on the verge of death because they are being shepherded by leaders who have little or no knowledge of what it means to live and lead under the presence and power of the Holy Spirit. The pastor who is Spirit filled will bring a type of sensitivity to the arena of church ministry that will make him a successful leader because he will be in close fellowship with God.

It is safe to say that many churches do not elect Spirit filled search committees for one of two reasons. **One**, they know little of the filling of the Holy Spirit or, **two**, they are deeply afraid of anyone who speaks about being filled with the Holy Spirit.

Putting Out the Fire

A pastor once related this fictitious story in a sermon about the Holy Spirit. The story is about two Neanderthal men who accidentally found fire. It was totally new to them. It was even a little frightening to them. They knew nothing about it but they discovered that it was a good thing. They realized the light given off by the fire made things better for them at night. They realized they could use it to cook food. They found that it kept them warm on very cold nights. As a result the fire brought their clan closer together as they discovered and used the qualities of the fire.

One day, because of carelessness, one of the Neanderthal men lost his home and his family to a terrible fire. As a result all the people discovered a bad quality in fire. It frightened them so badly that they gathered water and put out all the fires they had accumulated. Eventually, they had extinguished every fire in their camp. Because of their overreaction to the careless use of the fire they now lost all the enjoyment, comfort and help the fire, when used properly, had given them.

The pastor then applied the story in this way. He related that there was a day when the church had the fire of the Holy Spirit. But because of some flagrant and careless misuses of the wonderful Biblical truth of the **filling** of the **Holy Spirit**; the church, for all practical purposes, allowed its misplaced fear to extinguish the divine fire. The church must **regain** the Holy Spirit fire of the early church. The church must be awakened to the real need of Spirit filled leadership.

A Spirit powered search committee can do a much better job of insuring the church's future by seeking out and securing a prospective pastor who is filled with the Spirit and as a result lives a moral and ethical life. As the search committee seeks such a man of God they should check references, talk to denominational leaders and speak with former church members and other pastors who may know him. No question is out of bounds. Without leadership that is found blameless, the church has no hope of fulfilling its' God appointed purpose. It is a fact that there will be no **Holy Spirit powered churches** without **Spirit filled** leaders.

Fruits of the Spirit

Moreover, anyone who serves on the committee should be a person whose life exemplifies the **fruits** of the **Spirit** in their daily walk. One place in the New Testament where these are specifically enumerated is Galatians 5: 22 - 26. The congregation should be asked to carefully read and study this passage along with I Corinthians 13 before they undertake the task of electing a search committee. A person who feels spiritually unprepared to serve on the committee should never be pressured to serve and those who are appointed to the committee should surely understand the gravity of the task.

New Testament Terms

In the New Testament, three terms are applied to the office that we now refer to, generally, as pastor. One is the term Bishop (Episkopos -Επίσκοπος). Another is Elder (Presbuteros - Πρεσβυτερος). Back in the nineteenth century this term was widely used for the person who was occupying the office of pastor but today it usually refers to a group of laymen who basically serve as deacons or stewards. The third term is Pastor (Poimēn - Ποιμήν). This term basically describes a shepherd. The term Bishop describes one who is an **overseer**. The term Elder describes one who is basically a **minister**. The term pastor refers to one who "**leads the flock**". The modern pastor functions in all of these roles. For instance, in I Peter 5: 1 - 4 Peter charges: *"The elders who are among you I exhort, I who am a fellow elder and a witness of the sufferings of Christ, and also a partaker of the glory that will be revealed: **Shepherd the flock of God** which is among you, serving as **overseers**, not by constraint but willingly, not for dishonest gain but eagerly; nor as being lords over those entrusted to you, but being **examples to the flock**; and when the Chief Shepherd appears, you will receive the crown of glory that does not fade away."* It is clearly understood that Peter, under the **Spirit's** inspiration, sees the elders as functioning in the same way that a pastor would function. They are to be like shepherds who "**feed the flock of God**". In the position as Bishop, they will be taking "*the **oversight** thereof*". They are not to be men who do it simply for the sake of money (filthy lucre) but they are to do it willingly and they are to have a ready mind. They are to be strong **overseers** but **not dictators** and they are to serve in such a way as to be **examples** to the flock of fidelity to God's call. The term "pastor" also means shepherd. Peter sees the pastor as an undershepherd and states clearly that "*when the **Chief Shepherd** shall appear, ye shall receive a crown of glory that fadeth not away.*" The faithful pastor will receive the "*crown of glory*" (verse 4) that can never be taken away because it will **never fail**.

There currently seems to be a hazing of terminology here. It is clear from the Scriptures that the words for pastor, elder and bishop all refer to the same functional position in the church. Some churches have made grave mistakes by beginning an elder "ministry" in their church and appointing **the elders** as **overseers** of the pastor and his staff. One such church in its constitution and bylaws says: "The pastor and ministry staff shall be responsible to the elders of the church." This church has been counseled numerous times to remove that phrase from their documents but they have failed to do so. The church has been without a pastor now for four years. Some of the past candidates point out that part of the constitution and say "I'll never pastor a church with such an unbiblical view of pastoral leadership." The sad reality is that the so-called **"elder" ministry** has become another "**board**" much like the deacon "**board**." Some of the churches that have initiated an elder board are still in the dark about the infilling of the Holy Spirit. The elder board is just another step, in many instances, that hampers real Spirit filled ministry. It seems, in many cases, that such a board certainly does not help the church in becoming **Holy Spirit powered**!

Ephesian Elders

Paul stresses the same theme when he meets with the Elders of the Ephesian Church. He knew he would never see them again. His admonition was to "*… take heed to yourselves and to all the **flock**, among which the **Holy Spirit** has made you **overseers**, to shepherd the church of God which He purchased with His own blood. For I know this, that after my departure savage wolves will come in among you, not sparing the flock. Also from among yourselves men will rise up, speaking perverse things to draw away the disciples after themselves. Therefore watch, and remember that for three years I did not cease to warn everyone night and day with tears.*" (Acts

20: 28-31)   Here again the elders are to function as **overseers** and **pastors** who *"feed the church of God"*.   Who made them overseers?   It was the *"Holy Spirit"* who made them overseers (verse 28).   Again, we see that pastors are to be **Spirit powered** people and they cannot succeed *any other way*.   In Ephesians 4: 11-12 there is a listing of the various callings of God.   The list includes apostles, prophets, evangelists and **pastor/teachers**.   This makes it clear that a pastor is to be a teacher.   What is his task?   It is for the *"equipping of the saints for the work of ministry, for the edifying of the body of Christ, till we all come to the unity of the faith and the knowledge of the Son of God, to a perfect man, to the measure of the stature of the fullness of Christ; that we should no longer be children, tossed to and fro and carried about with every wind of doctrine, by the trickery of men, in the cunning craftiness by which they lie in wait to deceive, but speaking the truth in love, may grow up in all things into Him who is the head - Christ - …."* (verses 12 - 15)   This is a weighty assignment.   The term *"equipping of the saints"* means the maturing of the saints .   The pastor is to so lead the flock that they grow to maturity - that they are no longer babes in Christ.   This is what prepares them for the *"ministry"* (service) in the church and it leads to the *"edifying"* of the **body of Christ** which is the church.   So, it is the duty of the pastor, as the undershepherd, to so feed the flock on the word of God that they become mature Christians who can serve the church well which leads to the **edifying** or the *"building up"* of the church.   What an awesome task!!   This is thereason the pastor must be diligent or study to show himself approved or capable of rightly dividing the **word of truth** (II Timothy 2: 15).   A recent Barna survey found that many pastors struggle with articulating objectives for spirituality but instead prefer activities over attitude.   Among more than 600 pastors who were asked to identify Biblical references to chart a path to spiritual maturity for their flocks, only 2 percent listed the Galatians 5 passage which lists the **fruits of the Spirit.** So, how do we become *"full grown"* or *"complete"* so that our people become **spiritually mature**?   It is **through Christ** for, as Paul admonished the Colossians: *"… in Him dwells all the fullness of the Godhead bodily; and you are complete in Him, who is the head of all principality and power."* (Colossians 2: 9-10)

Qualifications

God, in His infinite wisdom, placed high qualifications on those leading the flock because their responsibility involves training other

Christians to live out the Christian life. All of the qualifications have to do with character and/or integrity. That character/integrity can only be possessed by a **Spirit powered** man of God. There are times when a church thrives simply because the pastor is **Spirit** filled even if some of the leaders know little about walking in the Spirit, but this is rare.

In the very recent past the American public has been bombarded with false prophets that, as their actions show, knew very little about living a Spirit filled life. We have witnessed the nationally known pastors who actually make a mockery of the pastoral ministry. Their showboat capers like asking God to "damn" America and becoming racial in the pulpit does irreparable damage to the image and influence of the church in American society. Instead of using the pulpit to preach the gospel they use the pulpit to promote their own small minded idea of politics. We can only wonder why their nonprofit status has never been brought into question.

Other televangelists who have bilked well meaning, kind but gullible, people out of millions of dollars in the "name of Jesus" have brought such a cloud over the pastoral ministry that it is more difficult to minister the **Word** in this present, anti-God environment.

Then, there was the heart breaking behavior of a widely known, pastor of a mega church and past president of the prestigious National Association of Evangelicals, coming clean about his sordid sexual encounters. Let us not forget a past President of the National Baptist Convention U.S.A. who sullied the good name of that denomination and was convicted of numerous felonies that brought disillusionment to so many. To be sure, these men have sought and received God's forgiveness but in a cynical world those things will never be forgotten by those who love to mock the church.

There are hundreds of ministers across denominational lines who fail morally every year that we never read about in the news media. With this kind of leadership in the pulpit, our churches are being filled with worldly ideas by worldly "pastors". Never before have we seen so many preachers of the Gospel fall to worldliness and lust.

This is a sad commentary on leaders and their commitment to being filled with the Spirit. If there was ever a time when churches ought to be seeking Spirit filled men to stand in their pulpits and preach the **Word,** it is now! The American public has been so inundated with bad press about pastors and distorted roles of the pastors' character in movies and television that the ministry is in dire straits. We must reclaim our position in American society with **Spirit powered**, **Godly** leaders in order to remove the false and distasteful connotation that pastors are uneducated, bumbling, scheming charlatans. There have always been the Balaams (Numbers 22: 21-33) and the Simons (Acts 8: 18 & 19) in the world. There always will be that kind, but let's not forget that the vast majority of pastors in America are good, upstanding men of God. Sad to say, however, many of them are struggling with their ministry because of the bad influence of those who have failed.

Much At Stake

Much is at stake for the church in these difficult days. As already pointed out, churches do not usually rise above their pastor. In fact many say that a church will take on the "persona" of their pastor's spirituality. If the pastor is worldly, the church will be worldly. If the pastor is careless in finances, the church will be also. For the church to accomplish what it must accomplish concerning the Great Commission, there must be massive change and that change must be spiritual. We don't need to change so much the way we **do** things as much as the **heart** of the **pastor** and the **church** must change.

There is also much at stake concerning the world as well. There is a saying…"As goes the pastor …so goes the church…as goes the church… so goes the world." Our world is snowballing toward evil and all the time unspiritual pastors are failing and unspiritual churches are failing. The salvation of the world depends upon the church leadership being **Spirit powered.**

For such an awesome task as the scriptures have assigned to the **Holy Spirit** filled pastor to lead the flock of God, there must be some very high qualifications. The passage most often used to describe those qualifications is found in I Timothy 3: 1-7. The term Bishop (Overseer) is used in that passage but, as we have stated earlier, it refers to the office of a pastor. The pastor must be "*blameless*". The word is translated from the Greek word, anepilepton (ανεπίληπτον). The word quite literally means "**irreproachable**". It also means "not open to censure" or one who "cannot be laid hold of". It basically refers to a man who has **character** and **integrity.** The word "integrity" means: uprightness of character and honesty. Where the character, integrity, and credibility of the pastor is lacking, that pastor's personal life must be repaired or he must remove himself from ministry. When a pastor is filled with the Spirit, his integrity and character will be evident in his walk with Christ.

The late Paul Harvey told a story that had to do with integrity. Four high school boys were late for class one morning. They entered the classroom very apologetically and told their teacher that they had been detained due to a flat tire. The teacher smiled and told them it was too bad because they had missed a test. The teacher said she was willing for them to make up the test on one condition. She gave each of them a piece of paper and pencil and sent them to the four corners of the room. She said, "You will pass the test if you can answer one question correctly: Which tire was flat?" What a real test of integrity! However, the pastor's integrity is being tested like that **every day**. We must pass the test or the world will hurt because of our failure.

The pastor is to be **guiltless** because he has been saved from sin through the shed blood of Jesus Christ at Calvary and he lives the Christian life with integrity. If he has no integrity he has **nothing!!** He is to be **monogamous**, that is, he is to be the husband of only one wife. To be sure, when a man has been widowed, he is free to remarry and still qualify for the ministry. In Matthew 19:9 Jesus gave the exception clause. He stated clearly that Moses allowed for divorcement only because of the hardness of their heart and then He reaffirmed that *"from the beginning it was **not so**."* The exception clause states clearly that divorce is allowable only for the cause of fornication which is a reference to lewd, deviate or un-natural sexual activity. Some believe that a man who has been through such a divorce, if he is the innocent party, is still eligible for the ministry but it seldom works out in a very practical way because most churches will not accept it.

A young pastor in a large city was taken by surprise when his wife of seven years called him to inform him she would not be home again. She was leaving him. This young man had completed his seminary work and had a fruitful ministry but now it was all falling apart. His deacons said they loved him and knew that the separation was not his fault but he could not continue to be their pastor. The difficulty he had in the past in ministry was nothing like he was about to experience. Even though the divorce was not his fault, he had to pay the consequences. He ended up being the pastor of a very small church that could not pay him a full time salary and he had to get a public job. Sad, isn't it? But, God's Word is true. Whether you have mixed feelings about this kind of situation or not, such a ministry will never be the same.

No Clowns

The one who would be **pastor** must be **sober**, **discreet** and **decorous**. The community clown may get a lot of **laughs** but he will not get much **respect**. It does not mean that the pastor cannot have a sense of humor but the pastor who is known for his "jokes" or for being a "practical joker" will not **succeed** in the ministry. He is to be a sober minded thinker and a person who is courteous and hospitable. He should be the kind of person who sets others at ease in his presence. He must also have a teacher's **aptitude**. While the pastor can, and should, cultivate the gift of teaching it is something that can only be conferred upon him by the **Holy Spirit**.

A Divine Call

Teaching the things of the Kingdom takes a teaching insight and discernment that can come from no other source than the **Spirit**. To be sure, college and seminary can certainly hone one's teaching ability but if the **Holy Spirit** has not conferred that ability upon a man it is likely that he has not received a **Divine call** to the ministry.

Merrill F. Unger in his book, *Principles of Expository Preaching says,* "In addition to an experience of regeneration and spiritual fullness resulting in the enjoyment of the Spirit's unobstructed teaching ministry, the Bible expositor must possess the settled conviction that **God has called and separated him to the gospel ministry as a life work.**" (Acts 13:2, Romans 1: 1) Some young men enter seminary with the idea of making ministry a profession. Ministry is not a "profession", it is a **divine call of God** to a special life of ministry that is set apart from others to do a particular type of ministry for the Kingdom of God. It **must not be viewed** as some type of chosen profession that anyone can fulfill. Other young men have entered seminary or the ministry because of the influence of a father or mother who really wanted their son to be in ministry. That is a noble desire but it can never take the place of the **divine call of God** to those young men.

Martyn Lloyd-Jones says in his book, *Preaching and Preachers,* "A preacher is not a Christian who decides to preach… He does not even decide to take up preaching as a calling… This picture of the type of life lived by the minister has often appealed to young men, and there have been many who have gone into the ministry in that way." He further states, "The answer to that false view is that preaching is never something that a man **decides** to do. What happens rather is that he becomes conscious of a **call**."

For one to put **himself** into ministry flies in the face of the **authority of God**. If my calling is of myself, my parents or the populace then where will I get the authority to carry out the ministry? There must be a **Divine call** in order for there to be **Divine authority**.

As stated earlier, in the callings listed in Ephesians 4: 11, the office of pastor is listed as a "*pastor/teacher*". Good **preaching** is also good **teaching**. There is no cleavage between the two. The preaching of the gospel is not a man "venting his spleen" or "getting something off his chest" but it is **expounding** the word of God and **applying** the teaching of the word of God to the lives of the people. When that happens, a Pastor has preached and no one can do it any better.

Skip the Wine

The pastor must also be a person who is "*not given to wine*". The key word there is **paroinon** (παροινον). Satan has surely destroyed many lives with alcohol and some of them have been pastors. There are so many ideas about the use of alcohol as a beverage but man's ideas don't really count. The worst problem with alcohol is the **influence it projects**. One would think that a pastor would know better than to drink alcohol. Sadly, some of them don't. One pastor of a prominent city church brags about having a wet bar in the parsonage and having deacons' meetings at his home so they can have a cocktail before their meeting. That is simply nonsense.

At this point it will be well to clarify the matter of wine as it is used in the New Testament. There are some who try to **justify** drinking alcoholic beverages because of the use of wine in the New Testament. There are no grounds for this. There are primarily two words that are translated "wine" in the New Testament. **One is gleukos** (γλεῦκος). That is the word that is used in Acts 2: 13. Some in Jerusalem were mocking the apostles who were speaking in other languages that they had not studied. Others were asking the meaning of what was happening. Some of the mockers had accused them of being "full of new wine". It is obvious that the term gleukos was referring to fermented wine and this is the **only time that the word is used in the New Testament**. When Peter began his message on the day of Pentecost he stated to the people that "*these are not drunk, as you suppose, since it is only the third hour of the day.*" (Acts 2:15) There could be no other logical conclusion but that gleukos refers to fermented wine with a sweetening agent that would make one drunk.

The **other** word that is often translated "wine" is **oinos** (οἶνος). This word is used 28 times in the New Testament and it usually refers simply to **grape juice or vinegar.** This is the term that was used in John 2: 9-10 where Jesus turned the water into wine at a wedding feast. This was the beginning of Jesus' miracles and obviously that "wine" did not have time to ferment. This is the same term that is used in I Timothy 3: 3-8. Some believe that the Timothy reference is a prohibition against the gluttonous use of wine (or juice) rather than the drunken use of it. In Matthew 9:17; Mark 2:22 and Luke 5:32 Jesus warns against putting fresh juice in old wine skins for fear it would cause quick fermentation and be ruined. Paul warns against the use of it in Romans 14: 21. Sometimes wine is referred to interchangeably as vinegar (compare Matthew 17: 34 and Mark 15: 23). While on the cross Jesus **refused** it! Christians will do well to heed Proverbs 23: 31 which warns of the destructive nature of fermented wine. The warning is that "..*it bites like a serpent, And stings like a viper.*" (Proverbs 23:32) It is necessary to deal with this issue because there are some new "thinkers" on the evangelical scene who contend that it is quite all right to go to a bar and have a drink with a person one is trying to win. There is no Biblical basis for that approach at all and it will ultimately lead to a loss of testimony and the death of any ministry. It is the clear teaching of the **Old and New Testament Scriptures** that the people of God were to reject alcoholic drinks. A qualification of the **Levitical priests** stated that they are not to be taken with "*wine or strong drink*" (Leviticus 10:9). Likewise, the **Nazarites**, "*shall separate himself from wine and similar drink; he shall drink neither vinegar made from wine nor vinegar made from similar drink; ...*" (Numbers 6:3) The bottom line is that the Scriptures are clear; the man of God must avoid alcohol **altogether!**

No Striker

Then follows the term "*not violent*" which has the connotation of a behavior that is abusive, and often associated with drinking strong drink. It often leads to violence and harm to others. Some scholars believe it refers to some type of gambling but the etymology of the word gives no hint of that. The Spirit filled pastor will not have a fighting spirit. A young pastor had just finished his third month in his new church field. There was one deacon who had never liked the young man from the first sermon he had delivered in the church. A real personality conflict arose between the two and a church battle ensued. The deacon did everything he could to agitate the pastor and the pastor did everything he could to alienate the deacon. One Sunday evening after the evening sermon the pastor called the church into conference and asked if there was any new business to be brought before the church. Knowing that the deacon had been getting his information together and gathering support, the pastor was afraid that the deacon would ask for his resignation. After the question was asked the deacon stood and walked toward the pulpit and said: "Preacher, I have something I need to say." The pastor said: "NO! You will not use my pulpit to stir up strife." The deacon continued his walk toward the pulpit and stepped up on the podium. The pastor continuously objected to his desire to speak. The deacon pushed his way behind the pulpit and when he did the pastor pushed back. A scuffle ensued and the pastor almost tore the shirt off the deacon. The other deacons had to break up a physical pushing and shoving match that took place in the pulpit. Granted, the deacon was wrong. He should not have pushed the issue in public. He should have taken other deacons to the pastor to try to work things out but the tragedy was the response of the pastor. No Spirit filled pastor would respond in such a manner when thrust into a bad situation. A Spirit filled pastor will always act in a Godly way even when threatened by physical harm.

Money

The Pastor also is to be one who is *"not greedy of money"*. This is a reference to money that is ill gotten or base in its origin. Many a reprobate has tried to "buy" a clear conscience by giving money to a pastor. In Acts 8:18 there is a record of Simon the sorcerer who feigned a belief in Jesus Christ. When he saw the miracles and wonders that were performed by the apostles with the laying on of hands, he offered them money if they would confer upon him the power of the **Holy Spirit.** Peter's answer was: *"… 'Your money perish with you, because you thought that the gift of God could be purchased with money! You have neither part nor portion in this matter, for your heart is not right in the sight of God. Repent therefore of this your wickedness, and pray God if perhaps the thought of your heart may be forgiven you.'"* (Acts 8: 18 - 22 V) No wonder Peter had such great power in his ministry and in his preaching!! While he was open to needed change, such as the preaching of the gospel to the gentiles, he would **never**

compromise the gospel message. He was not about to allow his life and ministry to be tainted with ill gotten money .

Moreover, the pastor is to be a calm and patient person who is not contentious. This has to do with temperament. He is not the kind of person who will "fly off the handle" and in a fit of rage, perhaps harm someone else. That is the reason the Scripture states that he is not to be a **drunken brawler** (paroinos, παροινοσ; connotes drunkenness). He is a person who has his temper well under control because he realizes the destructiveness of an uncontrolled temper. In addition, he is not guilty of the besetting sin of **covetousness** which is a transgression of one of the ten commandments. It is an uncontrolled yearning for something or someone that cannot be rightly obtained. He just does not love the things of the world.

Family

The pastor must be one who rules his own house **well**. This has to do with managing the affairs of his own family. This Scripture has the connotation of a man who is authoritative but not "bossy". His own children must be under "subjection" which means they respect his authority but he doesn't abuse them. This is a "tight rope" for any pastor to walk because there are many communities and churches who hold the pastor's children to much different standards than they hold for their own children. Many churches have those individuals in them who just love to "tattle" on the pastor's children and sometimes their "tattling" is gleaned from unreliable sources who have told a lie about the pastor's children to begin with. There are also those twisted individuals in churches who are willing to blame the influence of the pastor's children for the waywardness of their own children. The pastor must deal with his children and manage his family with "gravity" which indicates seriousness. He is their parent - not their pal.

On the other hand, ministry can be very hard on pastor's children. Children are quite observant. They know when their dad is being criticized and being hurt by someone in the church. They see their dad struggle with controlling his emotions in difficult situations and sometimes failing in his efforts. One thing is sure; they get a "bird's eye" view of hypocrisy in the church and they are harmed by it. As a result, some pastors' children leave home and church when they come of age and never attend church again.

Often a pastor may sacrifice his children for the church. This should **never happen**. Pastors' children need a dad just like every other child.

The unspoken rule for every pastor should be that his **day off** be **guarded** and **protected**. The church people should be informed that the pastor should only be bothered on that day only in cases of emergency. E-mail should be unchecked and all talk about work should cease. The pastor's day off should be the families day and no one else's.

The pastor's first obligation should be to his family and the **Spirit filled** man of God will take care of his family and spend time leading and loving them before he leads and loves the flock.

It is also true that many churches have unrealistic expectations of the pastor's wife. Many times, the pastor's wife must take a job in the secular world in order to "make ends meet". While the pastor's wife must be an enthusiastic supporter of his ministry, churches must always recognize that she is not some kind of glorified "wonder woman" who can take care of her family and do multiple things in the church. She will be a part of his "discreteness". There are times when she will need to be in the vicinity when he is counseling ladies. There are certain visitation situations that the pastor should not go into without **his wife at his side**. This may, sometimes, appear to be overly cautious but it will prevent a lot of heartache, grief and false accusations. The Scripture is clear. If a pastor cannot manage his own house well, he will not be able to manage the affairs of the church.

Not a Novice

The pastor should have some experience in living the Christian life before he is ordained to the Office of Pastor. The term "novice" refers to a new Christian or a new convert (I Timothy 3:6). There must be a time for other Christians to observe his life and see how he is maturing in the faith before he is ordained to the ministry. Above all, there must be that sense of **divine call**. Many times young men observe an effective pastor who has great influence, prominence and respect in the church and community . They want that prominence more than they want to proclaim the Gospel. Thus, young men are sometimes confused in the matter of their "call" to the ministry. That is when they can become "puffed up with pride" and "fall into the same condemnation as the devil". It is always sad and heart breaking when this happens in the life of a young pastor. The young pastor must also "have a good testimony among those who are on the outside." The pastor who has met all the other qualifications listed in this Step will, of course, have a good report of those on the outside. That means that he has so lived his life that no one can honestly report any reckless or un-Godly behavior in his life. This goes back to the matter of "being irreproachable" or "of good behavior". This kind of mature Christian will not "*fall into reproach and the snare of the devil.*" (I Timothy 3:7)

Our seminaries are churning out pastors annually. The problem is that close to half of them will not stay in ministry. Many come out of seminary into the local church with visions of grandeur and higher than normal expectations for their congregations. Many come fresh out of seminary with the idea that everything about the traditional church is wrong and, as a result, they seek to right the wrong. Then the trouble begins. A pastor that is new to the ministry ought to spend much time with a seasoned pastor to begin to understand the real aspects of ministry. Some novice pastors are coming fresh out of seminary with the idea that they can take a small town or country church and turn it into a "mega" church even though there is obviously not enough population in the area to support one. **It will not happen!** A seasoned, Spirit filled pastor will take a church **where it is** and lead it to greater heights in serving the Lord. A Spirit filled pastor will take time to learn the people and understand them. Then he will be able to lead them. Then, in those difficult hours when that pastor is so exhausted and feels bedraggled and befuddled; when he staggers under the burden; our Lord is always there to walk that second mile with him. That is His promise (Matthew 28: 20).

Deacons

The next group of leaders who must be **Spirit filled** is the body of deacons or elders. The section of I Timothy 3: 8-13 begins with the term "*likewise*". It means "*in like manner*". It means that the same basic moral qualifications that apply to the pastor also apply to the deacon. The deacon is to be **reverent.** That means that he is to be serious about his faith in Jesus Christ, and the body of Christ which is the church. He inspires reverence without being unapproachable. He is not to be "***double tongued***". That is, he is not to say one thing to a person's face and another to his back. He is not to be a gossip. He is not to be duplistic. He is to be a man who stands by his word. He doesn't give his word in a meeting of deacons and then change his mind after he talks to his wife or some critic of the church. He is the kind of man whom others can "tie to".

He is not a man who can be intimidated. When he has taken the right position he will stand by it. The deacon is not to be a drinker just as the pastor is not.

Like the pastor, he is not a **greedy person** who is **obsessed with money** or ill gotten gain. He is not the kind of man who cuts shady deals and excuses it by saying "It's just business." Neither will he excuse such actions by saying, "Everyone else does it." He has **integrity** and back bone about him. He is a good steward of his resources and he uses his resources in a spiritual manner. A deacon should always set an example of giving by giving at least a **tithe** of his income to the work of the Lord. The deacon is one who sincerely holds to the deep understandings of the Kingdom of God, "a mystery" that the world in general cannot understand. He is not a pretender. He holds the faith in a "**pure conscience**". The deacon must also be blameless or **unimpeachable** in his character. It is so important that these men must "*first be proved*" and then they are to serve in the office in an unimpeachable manner. The office of deacon is no place for a novice, or one who "**promises to do better**". A man who cannot or is unwilling to lead in public prayer or teach does not need to be a deacon.

Their wives must also be **reverent** or sincere in their faith. They are not to participate in slander but they are to be serious and faithful in all things. The deacons are also to be "*a one woman's man*" and manage their own houses well.

Nature of Service

The word deacon is translated from the Greek word diakonos (δίακονος). The term is a derivative of the ancient Greek word dioko (διoκo). It literally meant "one who stirs up dust". It was used to describe a runner and was later used to describe a household servant. Sometime after the church came into being on the Day of Pentecost; it was used to describe servants of the church. Sometimes it was used to describe civil servants or government employees. While the term "deacon" does not appear in Acts 6: 1-6, most scholars agree that the **office of deacon** grew out of the selection of "the **seven**". While the office of deacon carries with it similar qualifications to that of the pastor there is a distinct difference in the office. Pastors and preachers of the Gospel are men who have a **divine call** whereas deacons are **selected** by their fellow Christians in the church. In Acts 13: 2 we have the record of the **Holy Spirit** speaking to the church at Antioch as they ministered and fasted saying: "*... separate* to Me Barnabas and Saul for the work to which I have **called** them." The church fasted, prayed and laid hands on them. Today we refer to such activity as **ordination**. Then they sent them away on their missionary journey. While Paul had been called on the Damascus Road, he and Barnabas received a **special call** to carry out the Great Commission in witnessing to the "*uttermost part of the earth*". The pastor is one who has received a special divine call to a special mission just as did Paul and Barnabas. Of course, there is the record in the New Testament of Jesus calling His disciples or "*the Twelve*" which was a **special calling**. Eleven of them would eventually become apostles and Paul would become the twelfth apostle. Paul refers to himself in Romans 1: 1 as one "*called to be an apostle*".

Not only does the Holy Spirit issue special callings to the man of God but he sometimes restrains the man of God from doing things that would be a mistake. Just before Paul received the Macedonian call, he desired to go to Asia but the **Holy Spirit** forbad him. He and Silas then wanted to preach in Bithynia but the **Holy Spirit** "*did not permit them.*" (Acts 16: 6-7) After this they went to Troas. That night he had a vision in which he saw a man standing before him saying, "*come over to Macedonia and help us.*" After he saw the vision he endeavored immediately to go to Macedonia and the testimony of Scripture was: "*… immediately we sought to go to Macedonia, concluding that the Lord had called us to preach the gospel to them.*" (Acts 16: 9-10) Wherever Paul went to preach the gospel he went "*bound in the Spirit*". He later announced to the Ephesian elders that he would go "*bound in the spirit to Jerusalem, not knowing the things that will happen to me there, except that the **Holy Spirit** testifies in every city, saying that chains and tribulations await me.*" (Acts 20:22-23) But, Paul had already processed that. The Holy Spirit revealed to him what would happen there but that he was to go anyway. His response was: "*none of these things move me,; nor do I count my life dear to myself, so that I may finish my race with joy; and the ministry which I received from the Lord Jesus to testify to the gospel of the grace of God.*" (Acts 20: 24). Sometimes the Holy Spirit does not assign us easy tasks but we have the Lord's guarantee that he will be with us in our service to Him (Matthew 28: 20). In his greatest peril, the Apostle Paul was assured that he would preach the gospel in Rome and he did so for two years while he was under house arrest (Acts 28: 30-31).

The Seven

The selecting of the *"Seven"* in the Jerusalem Church came at a time when the Church had experienced very, very rapid growth. On the Day of Pentecost *"about 3,000 souls"* were added to the church (Acts 2: 41). When Peter preached on Solomon's Porch there were about 5,000 men saved (Acts 4: 4). There are statements like that which appeared in Acts 2: 47 that *"the Lord added to the church daily those who were being saved."* In Acts 5: 14 the Scripture tells us that *"believers were increasingly added to the Lord, multitudes of both men and women."* The church became so large that the apostles could not manage the daily distributions. Being under severe persecution, the people in the church had all things in common. They pooled their resources and the apostles distributed to the families according to their needs. The distribution became overwhelming *"when the number of the disciples was **multiplying.**"* (Acts 6:1) There arose a murmuring among the Grecian widows because they were being neglected in the daily ministration. The apostles called upon the church to *"seek out from among you seven men of good reputation, full of the **Holy Spirit** and **wisdom**, whom we may appoint over this business."* (Acts 6: 3) Why did they do this? So that they may give themselves to *"**prayer**, and to the ministry of the **word.**"* (Acts 6: 4) All seven of the men had Greek names and it can be safely assumed that they were Grecian men who were called upon to minister to the Grecian widows. Some have contended that these seven were indigenous pastors. That is likely a stretch that cannot be supported from the Scripture even though they did function as assistants to the apostles as well as servants of the church.

Witnessing Deacons

Among the seven were Stephen who would be martyred and Phillip who participated in the revival in Samaria and later witnessed to the Ethiopian Eunuch who had been up to the temple to worship. Phillip baptized him where there was *"much water"* and he went on his way rejoicing. We see then that the first deacons' earliest job was that of serving tables but it did not end there. They became **witnesses**. The word used in Acts 1:8 for witness is martures (μαρτυρες) from which our word "martyr" comes. It means to **bear testimony unto death**. Stephen bore witness unto his death. When Phillip left the revival in Samaria and went down south toward Gaza, he witnessed to the Eunuch who was reading from the fifty-third chapter of Isaiah. The etymology of the word "**deacon**" is that they first "*served tables*" or took care of the charity work. This is a task that deacons should always care for. Then, they were **witnesses**. The fact that believers were "*multiplied*" in Jerusalem suggests to us that the seven had a lot to do with it and they were **selected** because they were of "*good reputation, full of the **Holy Spirit** and wisdom.*" (Acts 6:3) They were to relieve the Apostles of the burden of distribution so that they could get back to "*prayer and the ministry of the word.*" Stephen gives us a glimpse into some of their witnessing activities. The Scripture tells us that he was "*full of faith and power did great wonders and signs among the people.*" (Acts 6: 8) Not only should deacons meet the qualifications set forth in I Timothy 3: 8 - 13, they should also be "*full of the **Holy Spirit** and **wisdom***" as well as being men of "***honest report***". Who should serve as deacons? Deacons should be men who are of honest report who are full of the **Holy Spirit** and wisdom!

A Blessing to the Pastor

The pastor is greatly blessed if he has Godly deacons. He is horribly cursed if he has deacons who see themselves as anything more than servants of the church. A Spirit filled deacon will love the Lord, the word of God and his pastor. When the pastor stands to preach the Word of God it is a great help and comfort for him to see **Spirit filled deacons** in the worship service supporting him. The Spirit filled deacon should pray for the pastor and share his vision for the church. He should be **supportive** of and **involved** in the evangelistic efforts of the church.

The Spirit filled pastor **needs** Spirit filled deacons. They should be men who understand the stress that the pastor and his family are under. They should be men who expect no more out of the pastor's children or wife than they expect of their own.

Hurtful Deacons

Seth is a bright and enthusiastic young man who grew up in a pastor's home but neither he nor his wife attend church regularly. While growing up in a pastor's home Seth sat in a Sunday School class that was taught by one of the leading deacons in the church. He owned a very lucrative business in the community that was known for the gossip that flowed freely through it, most of which centered on pastors and churches. This deacon/Sunday School teacher was so bold that at times he would gossip about Seth's father in his class of young people on Sunday mornings. Seth saw firsthand the **hypocrisy** of this deacon. He saw how mean spirited and void of any spirituality this deacon was and it left an indelible mark on him. As a result, Seth refuses to participate in a local church again. This story can be multiplied time and again. Careless, unspiritual deacons can do more harm to the pastor's children than any other situation in the church. A deacon should be very careful how he handles the man of God and his family because he will give an account before a **Holy God**.

Pastor's need men who will not try to usurp his God given leadership. Sometimes deacons see themselves, not as servants, but as slave masters who rule and oversee the pastor. This is not Biblical. The deacon in the local church is not a prestigious position, neither is it a position of authority, rather a Spirit filled deacon will see his position for what it is, a **servant**.

Some churches make a grave, unbiblical mistake by giving authority to the deacons that the Scripture never gives. They should never be allowed to control the finances of the church. They should never be given the right to give spiritual direction to the church. Neither should they be given any authority that would threaten the ministry and work of the pastor. Let the deacon be what God intended him to be, **a servant**!

Some Things Deacons Are Not

The office of deacon is an office that is much misunderstood, distorted and sometimes abused. The deacons are not a "board of directors". They are not supervisors of the pastor. They do not call and dismiss pastors. They are not to be the recipients of gossip. They are not there to take abuse. They are spiritual **servants** of the **church**. The deacons of today should take care of the charity work of the church. They should lead the congregation out into the community as witnesses of Jesus Christ. Whether a church uses the elder system or the deacon system, these men have a very special duty. It was James, the Brother of Jesus, who posed these questions: *"Is anyone among you sick? Let him call for the elders of the church, and let them pray over him, anointing him with oil in the name of the Lord."* (James 5: 14) An elder or deacon should not be ordained because he has money. He should not be ordained because he comes from a prominent family. He should not be ordained because his wife or his family want him to be ordained. He should be ordained only if he meets the spiritual qualifications that we have discussed and that are boldly set forth in the Scriptures.

Any deacon that seeks to humiliate his pastor is not **Spirit powered**. Sometimes the least spiritual men in the church are elected to serve as deacons. That will always cause major problems for the pastor and the church. It is clear that a church must have a Spirit filled pastor but it is just as important to have Spirit filled deacons.

A church that has Spirit powered men of wisdom who are sincere in their faith, committed to their Lord, who have a reputation of integrity, and a good deportment in the community will be a church that accomplishes great things for God. That church has reason to rejoice.

Other Teachers

The **Spirit powered church** must have Spirit filled people, not only in the office of pastor, elders or deacons, but the other teachers and leaders in the church must also be **Spirit powered** and must also be held to a high standard. With the founding of the Sunday School movement by Robert Raikes around 1780, there was a great expansion of Christian education in the local church. It met the need of small group Bible study. Later age graded Sunday School allowed **families** to attend Bible study in small groups of their own age. The Sunday Schools were so organized that parents could attend small group Bible study while their infant children were cared for in nurseries. Churches built large educational buildings which were another sign of their commitment to small group Bible study in the church. Various programs were developed to train Sunday School teachers and other workers. The Sunday School became an evangelistic arm of the church. At one time, 95% of baptisms in the local church came by way of the Sunday School. They were enrolled in the Sunday School before they were converted and became members of the church. The Sunday School became a great outreach program for the growth of local churches. This was true, especially in America. Christian leaders from across the world who visited America were amazed at what they called the "palatial church facilities" that they found in America. Seminaries established schools of religious education to train God called, Spirit filled educators to organize and grow great Sunday Schools. The Sunday School also provided a great financial stability for the church because most of a church's offerings came through the Sunday School.

Spiritual Leaders

While the Sunday School movement has been used mightily of God to grow some great churches, it is at this point that many churches became lax in their selection of the spiritual leadership for the church. While Bible teaching by the laity has brought great growth to churches, it has been accompanied by problems that could have been avoided if the church had also made sure that the teachers were Spirit filled people. Lay Bible teachers have been around for a long time but the movement was never so explosive as it was in America near the end of the Nineteenth Century and for most of the Twentieth Century.

A Sunday School teacher who is not **Spirit filled** cannot properly teach the Word of God. It is amazing how often the church will place new, baby Christians in positions of teaching simply because they don't have enough teachers to go around. Rather than placing new Christians in teaching positions, the church should have larger classes if necessary. A baby Christian knows nothing but the "milk" of the Word and is incapable of teaching effectively. Allowing this will almost always secure failure in the classroom. The Sunday School teacher is actually an arm of the pastor's teaching ministry and the Spirit filled pastor should always have input into who teaches in the Sunday School. It is safe to say that because of the pastor's God appointed position he will be ultimately responsible to God for what is taught in the church. If that is the case then he should have much to say about who teaches. That is the reason that pastors should always implement a continuous training program to train Sunday School teachers.

The Scriptures do not condemn Bible teaching by the laity but they urge caution. In James 3: 1, the earthly brother of Jesus cautions: *"… let not many of you become teachers."* He warns that teachers, in the Judgment, will be judged more strictly than others. He used the terms "we" which included himself. He is simply saying that not everyone needs to be a teacher. Teachers were then and are now very highly respected people. It is a position of honor and others tend to listen to and be influenced by one who is a teacher. This carries with it great responsibility. He continues in the chapter to warn believers of how destructive an unbridled tongue that is used carelessly and indiscreetly can become.

Paul's Warning

When Paul gave his farewell address to the Ephesian Elders he warned that "*after my departure savage wolves will come in among you, not sparing the flock. Also from among yourselves men will rise up, speaking perverse things, to draw away the disciples after themselves.*" (Acts 20: 29-30)   His advice to them was "*watch*".   Sometimes teaching positions become attractive to Godless men and women who seek influence in the church to become power brokers.   Such people will often try to develop "a church within a church".   We have even known of such classes moving out of the church to the Court House to be taught by some self-centered, or narcissistic Judge or some other official with standing in the community.   This became very prominent back in the thirties and forties, especially in small towns. Sometimes such classes form their own treasury and give only a portion of their treasury to the church.   The church should always make it clear that the **Sunday School** is **operated** by the **church** and that it is never to be an entity unto itself but it is **always** a part of the church and the teachers should **always** be elected by the **church**.

Jesus

Jesus warned about people who "... *love the best places at feasts, the best seats in the synagogues, greetings in the marketplaces, and to be called by men, 'Rabbi, Rabbi'.*"(Matthew 23 6-7)   His instruction was "*But you, do not be called 'Rabbi'; for One is your Teacher, the Christ, and you are all* **brethren**." (Matthew 23:8)   He also taught that the term "*Father*" was reserved to address the Heavenly Father in prayer and was not to be used to address earthly leaders.   He also **repeated**: "*..do not be called teachers; for One is your Teacher, the Christ.*" (Matthew 23: 10)   The fact that He **repeated** what He had said in verse 8 tells us how important this teaching is.   His warning was that: "*he who is greatest among you shall be your* **servant**. *And whoever* **exalts himself** *will be abased, and he who* **humbles** *himself will be* **exalted**." (Matthew 23: 11-12)   To some of the Pharisees in Jesus' day ostentatiousness was more important to them than humility.   The term, "Rabbi" and "Master" often referred to the same kind of person.   The teaching of Jesus is that the person who wants to be a great teacher will be humble and because he is humble he will be a successful teacher who will be exalted.   **Unfortunately**, there are always some people around who are just like those Scribes and Pharisees.   They want to use the church for their own personal agenda. Jude warns about this type. He compares them to Cain, the murderer and to Korah who was the one who led rebellion against God's chosen leaders (Moses and Aaron). He and some of his *"men of renown"* told Moses that they didn't need his leadership (Numbers 16: 1-40). Jude, the half brother of Jesus, was active in the early church at Jerusalem. He warns of men who have *"crept in unawares"* (verse 4). In verse 12 he compares them to *"clouds without water carried about of wind"*. In verse 16 he charges that they are *"murmurers"* and *"complainers, walking after their own lusts"*.

Examples

John had problems with a man by the name of Diotrephes (III John verses 9-10). He is described as one who *"loves to have the pre-eminence"*. He had apparently become a self styled dictator in the church and would not even receive a communication from apostles and would cast out of the church those who did want to receive communication from the apostles. Repeatedly, the New Testament warns against false teachers. Paul left Timothy at Ephesus so that he may *"charge some that they teach no other doctrine"* (I Timothy 1: 3-4). How were the early apostles and Christians warned of apostates and false teachers? It was the *"**Spirit**"* that would warn them. Paul said that the **Spirit** *"expressly says that in latter times some will depart from the faith, giving heed to **deceiving spirits** and **doctrines of demons**."* (I Timothy 4: 1) What will they do? They will speak *"lies in hypocrisy, having their own conscience seared with a hot iron."* We could continue at length with examples from the Scriptures regarding false teachers. They all have one thing in common. They know nothing of the **fullness** of the **Holy Spirit**.

Some churches are not careful enough about who teaches in the Sunday School or in other venues. On any given Sunday much false doctrine is taught in churches and, sadly, the church leaders do not realize it. If a teacher is not **Spirit filled** they may teach anything. One pastor recounts his experience in walking past one of his older women's classes and something caught his attention. The teacher was using Oprah Winfrey as her teaching source. He stood at the door and listened to the teacher speak glowingly about "Oprahisms" and praised her for her knowledge and wisdom. Well, it really doesn't matter what you think of Oprah. Sunday School is no place to be quoting her and using her ideas, especially when she espouses so much "new age" ideology and asserts that there are "many ways" to Heaven. We serve a Savior who states emphatically that **He** is *"the way, the truth and the life:* ***No one*** *comes to the* ***Father*** *except through* ***Me."*** (John 14: 6) The Sunday School class is no place to teach Dr. Phil, Oprah, or any other TV personality's views. Any gospel other than that found in the Bible is false. The Sunday School must have **Spirit powered** teachers who understand this or the church will not experience the blessings of God.

A pastor had accepted a new pastorate and had just moved on to the church field. The first week he was there, some men approached him demanding that he remove their Sunday School teacher. The new pastor didn't even know the teacher as yet. Naturally, he inquired as to why they wanted him to be removed. The answer was: "he is a drunk". Of course, the pastor inquired as to how such a man became teacher of a men's Sunday School class. The answer was: "he was not in church and we thought maybe it would get him in church". The men's class had ignored the nominating committee of the church and had elected their own teacher without church approval. It was a rebellious act from the start and yet, they wanted the new pastor to remove the teacher whom they had put in place in their rebellious act. Of course, when the man was removed he never came back to church. The church should have dealt with their rebellious act quickly and decisively but they "let it go". Some deacons told the pastor that they "just didn't want to make a stir". No one should ever be elected as a teacher for the purpose of "getting him in church". It never works and eventually will cause confusion and broken fellowship to some extent. The teachers should be **proven** and **respected** Christians before being elected.

The church nominating committee should always be made up of people who are guided by the **Holy Spirit** and the committee should always look for **Spirit filled** people to fill the teaching responsibilities in the church. How can this be determined? A Spirit filled person will always display the **fruits** of the **Spirit** in daily living. What are the fruits of the Spirit? The Scriptures make them quite clear. In Galatians 5: 22-23 they are enumerated which tells us that *"the fruit of the Spirit is love, joy, peace, long suffering, kindness, goodness, faithfulness, gentleness, self control. Against such there is no law."* The preceding verses list the works of the flesh and teach that the works of the flesh are always manifested in the life of a carnal person. A church that ignores these spiritual qualifications for teachers will often elect teachers with the worldly traits of people such as Melissa Hukabee who was charged with the murder and sexual molestation of a little eight year old neighbor girl, placed her body in a suitcase and threw her into a body of water. Every time the media announced it, they always stated that she was a Sunday School teacher. Christians across the nation were not only grieved but embarrassed by the tragedy. A committee that ignores the fruits of the Spirit in the lives of the people they elect to teaching positions will always bring chaos to a Church and they will render that church powerless if they don't completely destroy it. However, a committee that is **Spirit filled** and who have the fruits of the Spirit in their own lives will assure a church with **Spiritual power** that is **Spirit** driven. Spirit filled people will always be more conscientious about service. They will be dependable. We should never forget the old proverb that "the best ability is dependability". It is a congregation filled with people who have **fruit of the Spirit** in their lives that make for a great church. A Spirit filled congregation will be the result of a Spirit filled pastor leading Spirit filled deacons and Spirit filled Sunday School leaders! We all know of churches whose reputation and influence have been harmed by carnal leaders who knew nothing of the Spirit's guidance in the affairs of the church. These ungodly acts of church leaders have disillusioned many lost people who so desperately needed the witness of a Spirit filled church. The sad thing is that it need never happen if the church would establish Spiritual standards for leadership that are Biblically based.

POINTS FOR DISCUSSION

1. The congregation that desires a **Spirit powered church** must begin by seeking out and calling a **Spirit filled pastor**. No congregation will rise above the pastor. If the pastor is a Spirit filled man who desires a **Spirit powered church,** it can happen. If the pastor does not have a passion for the development of a Spirit powered church, it can never happen. Why is it so important that the pastor be Spirit filled?

2. The Pastor Search Committee should always consist of people who are guided by the **Holy Spirit** and who will look for a **Spirit filled** Pastor to fill the preaching and teaching responsibilities of the church. Why is this so important for the health of the church? How will the Spirit filled pastor affect the local church where he serves?

3. The church Deacon Ministry should always be made up of men who are guided by the **Holy Spirit**. Why should Deacons in the local church be Spirit led men? How can they help the church become a Spirit led and filled congregation?

4. The church nominating committee should always consist of people who are guided by the **Holy Spirit** and the committee should always look for **Spirit filled** people to fill the leadership roles and teaching responsibilities of the church. Does your church nominating committee operate in this way? If so, how? If not, why?

5. Do you agree with this statement "As goes the pastor ...so goes the church...as goes the church...so goes the world?" If you agree site evidence that makes it true?

6. Some churches are not careful enough about who teaches in Sunday school or in other teaching venues. On any given Sunday false doctrine is taught in churches and, sadly, the church leaders do not realize it. If a teacher is not **Spirit filled** they may teach faulty theology. How does your church make sure that the teachers are teaching the truth rather than false doctrine?

7. Discuss the importance of all church leadership being men and women who walk daily in the Spirit and seek to please God with their lives.

Step Five
Appropriate the Gifts of the Spirit

The **Spirit Powered Church** is a church of Spirit filled people with Spirit filled leadership who encourage the use of spiritual gifts. Dr. Elmer Towns gives an excellent definition of a spiritual gift in his book, *Analysis of the Gift of Faith in Church Growth*. He says: "A spiritual gift is spiritual in character (*pneumatikon*), sovereignly given by God the Holy Spirit (*charismata*), to minister to others (*diakonia*), in the power of God (*energema*), with an evident manifestation of the Holy Spirit through the Christian as he serves God (*phanerosis*)." The most commonly used passage concerning spiritual gifts is I Corinthians 12. There are also lists of spiritual gifts that appear in Romans 12: 6 - 8 and Ephesians 4: 8-11. The term spiritual gifts is translated from the Greek word pneumatikon (πνευματικῶν). This tells us that we are talking about gifts that can only be bestowed by the **Holy Spirit** of God. It is not gifts as the world sees gifts. We may admire athletes and sometimes men say of a person, "He is a gifted athlete." However, athletic skills are not **spiritual gifts**. We have all known athletes who could play a great game of football but they had no time for God at all. Sometimes, highly paid athletes commit crimes and are sent to prison because they have completely shut God out of their lives. We sometimes hear actors referred to as "gifted actors" who do despicable things in their personal lives. Sometimes musicians are referred to as "gifted musicians" who sing vulgar songs and commit the sleaziest kinds of immorality. To be sure, there are Christian athletes. There are Christian actors. There are Christian musicians. This is simply to point out that **physical skills** do not necessarily translate into **spiritual gifts**. It is to be remembered, however, that a person with physical skills may also possess spiritual gifts. Sometimes, even Christians are confused about this question. Sometimes, people who have physical skills and worldly knowledge are placed in places of leadership in the church because other Christians in the church have confused the two in their own minds. The person who has nothing but physical gifts or worldly acumen often gets those things confused with spiritual gifts in his own life. For instance, there are abundant illustrations of churches who feel that if there is a banker in their congregation, he must be the treasurer of the church even though he may not have any spiritual gifts. We have seen such situations in which such a person caused great grief in the church and they have been known to destroy the ministry of pastors. This is not to say that all bankers are that way. Some are good, Godly men who have spiritual vision. We have known of churches that would place an outstanding athlete who had no spiritual qualifications in a teaching position with young people. That always leads to disaster. Not every musician needs to play in church. Indeed, unless they have committed their musical talent to the glory of God they should not be asked to play or sing at all.

A pastor related his experience with a deacon who was constantly causing conflict. It was mostly over tiny financial matters. His by-word was, "We need to run the church like a business." Finally, the pastor understood that the man would ultimately break the fellowship of the church and he said to him: "The church is not a business. It is a ministry. A business is there for profit. The church is not here for profit. All the people give to this church is to be used in the ministry of the church." Happily, that deacon finally understood it and he became a good deacon as he gave control of his life to the **Holy Spirit**. It is our purpose in this chapter to discuss the various gifts of the Spirit in such a way that they can be clearly understood.

In the opening sentence of I Corinthians 12 Paul addresses spiritual gifts. As indicated above, the translation is from the Greek word, "pneumatikon." It literally means, "that which originates with God." We see then that spiritual gifts are not something that we can work up in the flesh no matter how much talent we have. Spiritual gifts depend entirely on our relationship with God. Again, they are administered by the Holy Spirit of God. We see this repeatedly in the lives of outstanding servants in the New Testament. While Paul waited in Athens for Silas and Timothy, "*his Spirit was provoked in him.*" This is just before he delivered the sermon on Mars Hill (Acts 17: 16). When the apostle John received the Revelation, he "*was in the **Spirit** on the Lord's day.*" (Revelation 1: 10) There are many other examples of this in the New Testament but these will suffice to illustrate our point. Paul points out in I Corinthians 12: 3 that the people need an understanding concerning Christ and that "*no man speaking by the Spirit of God calls Jesus accursed.*" He further points out that "*no one can say that Jesus is Lord except by the **Holy Spirit**.*" It must be clear when we discuss spiritual gifts that we have an understanding of their origin and their effect on the believer. In verses 4 - 6 of that chapter, we again have a discussion of the Trinity. There are diversities of gifts, differences of administration, and diversity of operations bestowed by the triune God and that spiritual gifts are given **not to exalt one individual** but to profit **everyone**. They are for the common good in the life of the church. The apostle prefaces the list of gifts by saying that they are *"given through the Spirit."* (Verse 8) The most important task of any nominating committee is to get the church leaders into the right position according to their **spiritual gifts.** Now we will look individually at the gifts.

Word of wisdom: The word of wisdom is translated from the Greek words, "logos sophias" (λόγος σοφιαζ). It means "**insight** into the **true nature** of things." This was a qualification for deacons. The apostles called upon the congregation in the church at Jerusalem to *"seek out from among you seven men of good reputation, full of the Holy Spirit and **wisdom**."* (Acts 5: 3)   Blessed is the church with a bountiful supply of men and women who have the gift of wisdom. Spirit filled deacns always have a settling affect on the church because they can discern ulterior motivations of those who would cause dissension and strife for the sake of their own personal agenda. People of wisdom can spot that type but they must also have the courage to confront them when they are wrong. They also realize how important it is to follow the leadership of a spirit led pastor and they will never display a **censorious spirit.**

Sensing Direction

People with the gift of wisdom can also discern the direction that a church ought to take in its' ministry whether it be a youth program, a musical program, an outreach program, a ministry program or a building program. There are times when personal workers may approach a lost person with the thought of winning them to Christ but they may discern that it is not the right time or place. There may be others, who would be a hindrance to the **working of the Holy Spirit**, present. The person may be in the midst of personal or family conflict. There are times when the soul winner must simply pay a friendly visit, making it brief, and come back later.   Sometimes, Christian people of wisdom have talked a person in distress out of doing something very foolish and harmful in their lives. It is sad but true that there are religious charlatans in every age who prey upon churches. They want to come to a church and draw off followers after themselves. Paul warned the elders of the church at Ephesus concerning this (Acts 20: 29-31). Paul referred to them as *"savage wolves"* and that they would not spare the flock. Paul warned that some of the elders themselves would rise up *"speaking perverse things, to draw away the disciples after themselves."* His advice to the elders was that they should *"watch, and remember that for three years I did not cease to warn everyone night and day with tears."*

Diotrephes

John's problem with a man named Diotrephes who *"loves to have the pre-eminence"* (III John 9) was similar. People of **wisdom** know that Satan never sleeps. Peter warned of *"false prophets"* and *"false teachers among you."* Peter charged that such people would bring in *"destructive heresies"* (II Peter 2: 1-2). The person of wisdom is always mindful of the warning of Peter himself that we should *"Be sober, be vigilant; because your adversary the devil walks about like a roaring lion, seeking whom he may devour."* (I Peter 5: 8) Peter's counsel is that we should *"resist him, steadfast in the faith."* (Verse 9) People of wisdom will often counsel immature Christians against taking harsh actions or speaking intemperate words in a time when they have been **"wounded in their Spirit."** They are the kind of people who believe in *"turning the other cheek."*

Vision

People of wisdom also have vision and they realize *"where there is no revelation, the people cast off restraint."* (Proverbs 29:18) The people of vision can always spot the seven deadly sins, which are *"a proud look, a lying tongue, hands that shed innocent blood, a heart that devises wicked plans, feet that are swift in running to evil, a false witness who speaks lies, and one who sows discord among brethren."* (Proverbs 6: 16 - 19) Moreover, people of wisdom can always spot the fruits of the Spirit because they are the people who *"walk in the Spirit"* (Galatians 5: 22-26). That passage also warns against *"becoming conceited, provoking one another, and envying one another."* People of **wisdom** have a great ability to keep the church focused on its' mission of taking the Gospel to the uttermost part of the world (Acts 1: 8). It is always true that people of **wisdom** are a **healing force** in the Church.

Not Human Intelligence

It is sometimes very easy for Christians to conclude, erroneously, that wisdom is a sign of human intelligence. This is not true. One writer says, "… *on the contrary true wisdom really is a moral quality.*" Churches must always remember that worldly wisdom or human wisdom is not equated with **Godly wisdom**. We all have known of very intelligent people who had very little wisdom. Likewise, some have wisdom with less intelligence than others. There is a story that floats around the state of South Carolina about a truck driver who got lost on some of the back roads of that state. He came to an intersection where five roads came together. He was very confused. There were not enough signs there to give him much instruction. He called to a little boy who was standing near the intersection and asked the little boy where each of the roads went. In each case the little boy replied, "I *don't know.*" The exasperated truck driver asked, "*Son, you just don't know much of anything do you?*" The little boy replied, "*No sir, but I am not lost.*" To be sure, the little boy may have been experientially lacking but he certainly was not lacking in the area of wit. He did have a certain wisdom.

True Wisdom

True wisdom always begins with living under the rule and power of the triune God. The scriptures have a word on the subject: "*the fear of the Lord is the beginning of wisdom: A good understanding have all those who do His commandments.*" (Psalms 111: 10) The difference between true wisdom and worldly or human wisdom is that true wisdom is of God and the other may well be satanic. Godly wisdom is what every pastor, teacher, deacon or leader needs since every individual and every church is different. An examination of two basic types of **wisdom** is apropos at this point.

Worldly Wisdom/Godly Wisdom

We often hear of people who are rude, cunning and clever referred to as being "*worldly wise.*" They could beat anyone at Poker. They can "*hose*" you in a trade. They are often said to be able to "*turn every situation into money.*" While they are often described as being "*worldly wise,*" it is not Godly wisdom. One of the short comings of worldly wisdom is recorded in Ecclesiastes 1: 16 - 18 which says: "*I communed with my heart, saying,*

'Look, I have attained greatness, and have gained more wisdom than all who were before me in Jerusalem. My heart has understood great wisdom and knowledge.' And I set my heart to know wisdom and to know madness and folly. I perceived that this also is grasping for the wind. For in much wisdom is much grief, and he who increases knowledge increases sorrow." Paul addresses worldly wisdom in I Corinthians 2: 6 when he says, "However, we speak wisdom among those who are mature, yet not the wisdom of this age, nor of the rulers of this age, who are coming to nothing." Paul further clarifies worldly wisdom when he said: "...the wisdom of this world is foolishness with God ..." (I Corinthians 3: 19)

The Functioning Church

A church cannot function properly from the wisdom of man or the wisdom of the world. Worldly wisdom originates in the human heart that is not in tune with God. This is the kind of wisdom that is associated with the idea of "*doing*" church like a business. The church cannot be operated like a secular business by secular rules of economics. It is always dangerous when a church makes enormous decisions based on the wisdom of some leader or group of leaders in the church who do not possess Godly wisdom. The church is a divine, living organism and cannot be a Spirit led church if it is not led by Spirit filled leaders. A church cannot be led by people of human wisdom if it is to accomplish the will of God in the world. Those with worldly wisdom cannot understand spiritual things. They will often try to gain wisdom by trying to imitate someone else and that someone else may lead them astray. Jesus warned about the blind leading the blind. Neither does wisdom necessarily come with age although it is often developed through years of experience. That is the reason that the New Testament church depended so much on "elders" that we discussed earlier. A younger Christian who stays in the word of God and spends time with God in prayer may develop just as much wisdom as one who is older and sometimes older people develop more stubbornness than wisdom.

Wisdom Of God

The apostle Paul speaks of "*those who are **mature**.*" (I Corinthians 2: 6) Paul continues by saying: "... *we speak the wisdom of God in a mystery, the hidden wisdom which God ordained before the ages for our glory.*" (I Corinthians 2: 7) Godly wisdom sees the church as God sees it. Paul is saying these things to the church at Corinth because the church had substituted human wisdom for Godly wisdom and the outcome was not good. Any church that operates from worldly wisdom will always suffer failure. Even though many of the members in the Corinthian church had experienced salvation in Christ, they still wanted to cling to some of their past pagan philosophies that were a detriment to the working of the Holy Spirit in the church. The result was division in the church. Sadly enough, that kind of division still happens in present day churches when we allow human wisdom to take the place of Godly wisdom. John Macarthur addresses it when he says; "... *philosophy; it is unnecessary. Why? Because when it is right it will agree with Scripture and when it is wrong it is unneeded.*"

In I Corinthians 1: 20 Paul poses the question: "*Where is the wise? Where is the scribe? Where is the disputer of this age? Has not God made foolish the **wisdom of this world**?*" He further reminded them that "*the world through wisdom did not know God*" (I Corinthians 1: 21) and that "*it pleased God by the foolishness of preaching to save them that believe.*" He made it clear that we preach "*Christ crucified, to the Jews a stumbling block, and to the Greeks foolishness, but to those who are called, both Jews and Greeks, Christ the power of God and the **wisdom of God**.*" (I Corinthians 1: 23 - 24) We learn, then, that the wisdom of God is far, far superior to the wisdom of the world; so much so that they can hardly be compared.

The Clincher

In Chapter 2 of I Corinthians Paul gave the clincher when he said: "*my speech and my preaching were not with persuasive words of **human wisdom**, but in demonstration of the **Spirit** and of power, that your faith should not be in the wisdom of men but in the power of God. However, we speak wisdom among those who are mature, yet not the wisdom of this age, nor of the rulers of this age, who are coming to nothing. But we speak the wisdom of God in a mystery, the hidden wisdom which God ordained before the ages for our glory.*" (I Corinthians 2: 4 - 7) In doing so, he gave the Corinthian church the perfect formula for putting their petty differences behind them and gaining the unity of the Spirit.

Where Do We Use Them?

People of wisdom should always be assigned to the decision making committees of the church because that is where churches most often go astray. For instance, the pastor search committee should always be occupied by men and women of wisdom. If that is not true, they will find the proper man of God for the church only by accident but the path of accident will seldom find the right person for the right position. Only people of proven wisdom should be ordained to the office of deacon. A deacon body filled with men of Godly wisdom can be of immeasurable help in the ministry of a church. Their decisions will be right and their support of church leadership will be most valuable. To ordain even one man to the office of deacon who does not possess **Godly wisdom** can wreak havoc in the church.

Nominations

The same applies to the nominating committee. Only people of Godly wisdom will be able to seek out God's people for leadership positions in the church. Other important committees such as the youth committee that oversees the activities of the youth must **always** be men and women of wisdom because only those people with Godly wisdom will be able to sense dangers when youth activities seem to be leading to opportunities for sinfulness and destruction for the young people. Several years ago a prominent church suffered national embarrassment because some of its' members had a Halloween party in a large hotel. The party got so out of control that furniture was tossed out of the rooms down into the atrium of the hotel. The police had to be called to break up the party. How could a thing like this happen? It was patently obvious that Godly wisdom had not been employed in the planning of that activity. There have been other examples in which young people have gone away to church camps or other church functions and brought girls back pregnant. When that kind of thing happens, it is obvious that wisdom has not guided the youth program. While many people in a church may possess more than one spiritual gift, it is always true that the people who are involved in selecting church leadership and planning church ministries should always possess the spiritual gift of wisdom above all else.

Word of knowledge: This term is translated from the Greek term logos ginoskos (λογος γινωσκως). This term carries with it the connotation of a comprehensive understanding and appreciation of the things of God and the actions of God. Such knowledge is the gift of God into the life of the believer. Such knowledge is not attained by mere intellectual activity but by the operation of the Holy Spirit after one's acceptance of Christ. It is not a knowledge that is marked by finality but that is constantly growing and ongoing. But what is the greatest knowledge in the world? The same word that we are using here was used by Paul in Philippians 3. Paul points out that he had attained high standing among the Jews. He was a *"Hebrew of Hebrews."* He had been circumcised on the eighth day. He was a Pharisee. He was so zealous for his faith that he persecuted the church. He had counted all those things that gave him station in life as but *"dung"*. Why? He gave the answer when he said: *"that I may **know Him**, and the power of His resurrection, and the fellowship of His suffering, being conformed to His death."* (Philippians 3: 10) It is the same word, "ginosko" (γινωσκο) used by Mary in the first chapter of Luke at the annunciation when the angel told her that she would conceive and bring forth a son and she was to call His name Jesus (Verse 31). Mary's question was: *"How can this be, since I do not **know** a man?"* (Verse 34) The angel made it clear that the Holy Spirit would come to her and the power of the **Highest** would overshadow and cause her to conceive even though she was a virgin and the child would be the holy child, Jesus. He would become the God/Man. The word **know** indicates that sacred moment when a husband and wife come together and become **one.** What is Paul saying? Paul is saying that is what happened to him **spiritually** on the **Damascus road** when Jesus appeared unto him, he and Jesus became **one spiritually**. They were bound together in Spirit forever. Eventually, Paul went over into Asia and there received a detailed account of the gospel of Jesus Christ. After three years he returned to Jerusalem where he conferred with the apostles. They found that the gospel which was delivered to him by the Holy Spirit in Arabia was identical to the gospel that Peter and the other apostles had preached (Galatians 1:11-2:10). Paul made it clear that he received the **knowledge** of the Gospel of Jesus Christ by **Divine revelation**.

My Conviction

It is the conviction of this writer that the **knowledge** of the gospel of Jesus Christ is the most critical and indispensable knowledge that any believer can possess. We have always been convinced that the most **sensible** people in the world are Christians and that the Holy Spirit is like a gyroscope in their lives that keeps them on an even keel and on **course**. At the end of his life Paul said, *"I have finished the **race**."* (II Timothy 4:7) This is the term (ginosko) that is used in John 8:32 where Jesus said, *"You shall **know** the **truth** and the truth shall **make you free**."* This kind of knowledge will make one free from the bondage of sin because *"If the Son makes you free, you shall be free indeed."* (John 8: 36) These are the kind of people who *"hunger and thirst for righteousness."* (Matthew 5: 6) Their knowledge is not a false knowledge but it is a **scriptural knowledge** and they are not easily carried about with every wind of doctrine. The promise of Jesus is that *"they shall be filled."* When they face problems in their lives they look for **scriptural** answers. When they give counsel to their brothers and sisters in Christ, it is **scriptural** counsel. They understand how to apply the principles of the scriptures in their own lives. These are people who have not only caught the Spirit of Christ but it is reflected in their conduct and their conversation. They can discern what is of God and what is not of God. These are the Christians who make outstanding Sunday School teachers and officers of the church.

Supernatural

Some have said that the "word of knowledge" is a "supernatural comprehension of Christ and His word." As has been stated before, the greatest knowledge that a human being can have is the knowledge that the God of the universe gave His only begotten Son to save sinners. Sadly, some churches seem to have stepped away from this knowledge for lesser knowledge. They presently tend to seek the knowledge of the world. Being "politically correct" seems to be more important to some church leaders and Christians than knowing the scriptures and living them in their daily lives. Knowledge is useless unless it is utilized. Our secular world would like to shut down the church's knowledge of spiritual things because the concepts that the church has been built upon for many centuries is a threat to a secular humanist/socialistic approach to life.

The church must arise and lay hold of scriptural knowledge and principles once again. Not the kind of knowledge the world deems important but the knowledge of the Word of God, Godly knowledge, which is scriptural knowledge, is the only knowledge that will change the world.

Avoid Precarious Concepts

Many would take the concept of "the word of knowledge" to a precarious point. Some would like to use the concept to claim to know the "secrets" of men's hearts. Christian beware! Only God knows a man's heart, certainly not other men. Men can only discern the fruits of a Godly life. Some would use it to tell others what God is saying to them. In a local church revival the visiting evangelist tried to say that he had the "gift of the word of knowledge" by telling people what God had said to him about their lives. The evangelist alienated a number of good Godly Christians because of his so-called "words of knowledge." He even told one of the women in the church that she had cancer and the cancer was there because of the judgment of God upon her life for living in adultery. To this day the woman does not have cancer and she remains a very Godly woman who loves the Lord and her church.

These types of ideas cloud the real purpose of the gifts that God said He has for us through the **Holy Spirit**. We have no doubt that God speaks to us in many different ways but He will never tell us about someone else's sin. His righteousness and holiness would not allow it! The word of knowledge is a gift for self understanding, self evaluation and self growth. It is also about situations we face, but it is not a "spiritual tool" that we use to examine others. That is the Holy Spirit's job. Let us leave that to Him. He is highly capable. A Spirit powered church must be a church that seeks to know God in an intimate way.

People who make up those committees that are involved in the selection of literature for the Sunday School, Mission organizations, youth groups, home bible studies and other study groups should certainly be gifted with the **word of knowledge**. These Christians understand real Biblical principles. For instance, because some Old Testament characters had multiple wives does not negate the clear teaching of monogamy that is so Biblical (Matthew 19: 4 - 6; Genesis 1:27). The Christian who is gifted with the **word of knowledge** understands these deep Biblical principles rather than forever searching for a "proof text" to support his own agenda or preferences.

Faith: Faith is translated from the word pistis (πιστις). It means a deep conviction held without reference to physical proof. This gift is given by "*the same Spirit.*" This is the kind of faith that Jesus talked to the disciples about in Matthew 17: 19. He had just come down from the mount of transfiguration. A man had brought a little epileptic boy to His disciples for healing. He had seizures that were sometimes so violent that they caused the boy to fall into fire and often into water. Physicians of that day did not understand much about the disease. Divine intervention was about the only hope of such patients. When Jesus came on to the scene the father of the boy said, *"I brought him to Your disciples, but they could not cure him"* (Matthew 17: 16) and he was right. The disciples **could not.** Why? Jesus gave them the answer. It was because they were **faithless.** There was a certain degree of unbelief on the part of the disciples. Jesus' word to them was that if they had the faith of a **grain of mustard seed** they could remove mountains. He also made it clear that nothing is impossible to those who have faith and who want to accomplish things for the glory of God. Faith is another gift of the Spirit. In Luke 17: 5 the apostles asked Jesus to *"increase our faith."* They understood Jesus' teaching on forgiveness and they understood that faith was connected to the ability to forgive. Even if a person trespasses against us seven times in a day and comes back to ask forgiveness then we are to forgive him seven times. The Apostles saw this as a difficult thing to do. That is when they asked Jesus to **increase** their faith. Again, Jesus used the metaphor of the mustard seed but this time the metaphor was used concerning a tree (Luke 17: 6). Of course, the apostles were saved by faith as we are also **saved by faith.** In the Acts of the apostles, all of their great undertakings and accomplishments for the Lord were accomplished through faith. When the lame man was healed, Peter made it clear that it was through **faith** in **His** name that the man was **made whole.** When Barnabas went to Antioch and saw the grace of God at work he began to exhort. The Scripture describes Barnabas as *"full of the Holy Spirit and of faith."* These two things go hand in hand. As a result of his faithful message the Bible says *"a great many people were added to the Lord."* (Acts 11: 24 NKJV) The scriptures make it clear that *"without faith it is impossible to please Him for he that comes to God must **believe** that **He is**, and that He is a rewarder of them who **diligently seek Him**."* (Hebrews 11: 6) We see then, that faith not only brings us to salvation but it is the catalyst in our lives by which we undertake the callings of God. Peter and John who lifted up the lame man in the name of Jesus and through **faith** in **His name** were among those disciples who pleaded with the Lord to *"increase our faith."*

A Catalyst

Faith is the catalyst that moves churches and the kingdom of God. We will never see a real church that was not built by faith. Faith and the **Holy Spirit** go hand in hand. It is only by the **Spirit and through faith** that we can undertake things for God. While there are diversities of gifts, Christians are not confined **to only one gift**. For instance, wisdom and knowledge are often coupled with faith (James 3: 13-18). In fact, faith touches about everything we can do in obedience to God because it can only be done as His **Holy Spirit** works through us. Every church can be thankful for those stalwart Christians who have an unshakable faith in His **Word**. They are not glory seekers nor do they attempt to flaunt their faith because they know that would not be pleasing to God as we learn in I Corinthians 13. They are those people who will be there Sunday after Sunday carrying out their duties. They may be teaching little children or adults. They may be ushers who work to keep the congregation orderly, safe and comfortable. They are always there to help in times of emergency. They are the ones who are always willing to **sacrifice** for the body of Christ when sacrifice is called for. They are there to minister in the name of Jesus during disastrous and critical times in the lives of the people. It is probably true that the greatest enemy of most Christians who feel helpless is their lack of faith or "*little faith*" as Jesus put it in Matthew 17.

Faith and Works

It is James who cautions us that faith is expressed not only in word but also by works. It is faith that strengthens us in times of trial. James reminds us that "*the testing of your faith produces **patience**.*" (James 1:3) He enjoins us to "*ask in faith, with no doubting, for he who doubts is like a wave of the sea driven and tossed by the wind.*" (James 1: 6) Faith is an indispensable ingredient in the life of anyone who would accomplish things in the name of the Triune God. That is the clear teaching of Hebrews 11, which defines faith in verse 1 as both **substance** and **evidence**. In other words, faith is not a leap in the dark.

The gift of faith is intrinsically important to having a Spirit powered church. Everything in the church is directly tied to the concept of faith. Without revisiting what faith is we now explore the absolute necessity of the gift of **faith** in the local church. One must understand that at the heart of **faith** is absolute surrender of the human heart and will to Christ.

119

The first application of the gift of faith in the local church is seen in the reality that faith is seeing the unseen, the invisible. Faith is making real what cannot be seen or sensed with human faculties. We find these words in Hebrews 11:1: *"Now faith is the **substance** of things hoped for, the **evidence** of things not seen."* For a church to be Spirit powered the pastor and its leaders must have this kind of faith. They must be willing to step out and try the seemingly **impossible** for the kingdom. When churches live by faith it morphs from the natural into the supernatural.

Second, when a church is living under the gift of faith it will step out into places where there is no step. Steven Spielberg's 1989 movie **Indiana Jones and the Last Crusade** tells the story of the pursuit of the holy grail of Christ. One scene in the movie shows Indiana Jones coming to a precipice where there seems to be no way across. The chasm was deep and dangerous. But, because of a riddle that spoke of faith when he came to that place he decided to take one step into the abyss and when he did a walkway appeared and he made his journey to the holy grail. That scene in the movie is a perfect picture of the kind of faith the church needs to have in these desperate days. The church, to be a Spirit powered church, must have the faith to step out into the invisible. A perfect example of this kind of faith is seen in the life of Moses leading the children across the Red Sea as he took one step into a dry sea bed.

Third, this kind of faith in the life of a Spirit powered church will bring power that goes beyond the natural abilities of man. Joshua at Jericho presents a beautiful picture of this kind of power that results from this faith. They obeyed God and had faith in Him and the walls were destroyed.

Fourth, this kind of faith and prayer go hand in hand. The more faith we have the more we will pray and the more we pray the more faith we will have. Any church that exhibits this gift of faith - real faith, will always be known as a praying church. The old adage is true, "You get your power while you are on your knees." This prayer life linked with faith brings victory to the Christian life and to the life of the church and helps overcome the obstacles that the world and the devil place in the pathway.

Believe The Word

This type of faith calls on the church to believe the Word of God above all human wisdom, doubt or criticism. This kind of faith always stands on the integrity of God and His promises. That is why it is so important that the church learn to trust the heavenly Father and live by faith in Him daily. This faith is a mystery. It is dynamic and powerful and most importantly, it connects us to Jesus our Lord (John 15).

The exercise of this faith and especially the results of the faith must always be that which brings attention to the Lord Jesus Christ for it is in Him that the power lies. The gift of faith is both a gift of God's grace and a human response to that gift.

One writer says that the Gift of Faith is "a special surge of God confidence." It is a time of trusting God to do certain things that a man cannot do. This is of great benefit to the believer and the church because it gives the ability for the Christian to have an attitude of Godly quests. Faith will always be a motivating factor in the Spirit powered church.

Healing: The gift of healing is always given to authenticate the Word of God. As there are various kinds of illnesses there are various kinds of healings. Sometimes God uses physicians in the healing process. Luke was a physician. There were certain medications they had in those days such as some herbs, ointments and purgatives.

There are few pastors who do not have a season of prayer every Lord's Day for those who are sick. Many people who are sick never go to a physician. Sometimes they use home remedies and sometimes they simply wait for the body to heal itself, which is miraculous in and of itself. Again, it is James who says: "*Is any among you **sick**? Let him call for the **elders of the church**, and let them pray over him, anointing him with oil in the name of the Lord. And the **prayer of faith** will save the sick, and the Lord will raise him up. And if he has committed sins, he will be forgiven.*" (James 5:14-15) Of course, as we have already pointed out in this book, our prayers are always to be conditioned to the **will of God**. Moreover, it is appointed unto man **once to die** and after that the judgment (Hebrews 9:27). The gift of healing is often found among women. There have always been women like Florence Nightingale who worked tirelessly to care for the hurt and the wounded. We must always recognize, however, that the gift of healing was not always given indiscriminately. Even the apostle Paul left Trophimus at Miletus sick (II Timothy 4:20). If Paul could have healed him, he surely would have. Even Paul had an infirmity that God did not heal but gave Paul grace to bear it (II Corinthians 12: 7-10). It is not the will of God that all people should be healed in every circumstance but we are thankful for those Christian physicians, nurses and paramedics who love God and work tirelessly to heal the sick. But, we must always remember that **all healing is of God**. The surgeon may "set the stage" for healing but it is the heavenly Father who causes those cells to knit back together and heal. While medications and antibiotics can diminish those things that prevent healing, it is always the work of God. Paul is careful to point out that healing comes by the same Spirit who bestows other gifts.

All healing is a divine gift. Whether it is brought about because of prayer or by medicine, it is divine. The concept of divine healing, however, has been perverted by modern day "faith healers" that would draw the attention away from God and place it on themselves and their "ministry". Any healing that takes place is the result of a power much greater than ours. It will always come from God and it can come in many different ways.

Areas of Healing

There are two areas of human existence that need healing. Often our physical bodies need healing so we pray and we ask God for healing. We often see a physician who applies his knowledge to our problem. Sometimes we are healed and sometimes we are not. God added fifteen years to Hezekiah's life after he **prayed** for God's **healing** (Isaiah 38: 1-6). Then there is the human spirit that needs healing. This healing is the most important healing. When we take part in the healing of a soul we help someone secure life for eternity. It is a real fact that no matter how much healing takes place in the human body, sooner or later there will be no healing and the body will die. Contrast this to the healing of the human soul that will **never die**.

This author believes in divine healing because he believes that all healing is divine. But, he believes that the greatest healing business the Spirit powered church can be involved in is the healing of the soul. Helping to apply the "soothing balm of Gilead" to the hurts of a lost soul is the most important healing of all (Jeremiah 8:22).

The Healing Process

Prayer coupled with the gift of healing plays an integral part in the healing process. Some recent medical journals have documented the power of prayer in the healing process. For centuries Christians have been praying for the sick with amazing results. This approach is completely Biblical and the Spirit powered church should have an ongoing ministry of prayer for the sick, but be aware that no man can lay hands on any sick person and heal them. Only God the creator of mankind has the power to heal. That is what we must pray for.

Not everyone will be healed. God sometimes uses our suffering for His glory as was the case of the man born blind that we read about in John 9:3. Sometimes He uses our suffering to mold us and shape us into His image. Living in this world is not easy. Life brings some grief and sorrow but God has a plan for us anyway. The Christian and the Spirit powered church must learn to rejoice when God chooses to heal and to persevere when He does not.

Some would argue that the position stated thus far says that God does not heal. On the contrary, God is the only one who can heal. Whether He chooses to heal through physicians, nurses, medicines, or the prayers of the saints does not matter. All healing is a gift from God. The Spirit powered church should be in the healing business. It must pray for the physically sick and win to Christ those who are sin sick. The faithful prayers of the Spirit powered church will be heard and answered.

Miracles: the greatest miracle of all - **salvation**!

Biblical miracles basically fall into two categories. There are physical miracles that involve the suspension of the natural order. There are spiritual miracles, which involve the metamorphosis of the spiritual life of an individual. Physical miracles, as recorded in scripture, are **rare** and **temporary**. There were some miracles surrounding the deliverance of Israel from the Egyptian bondage such as the ten plagues that culminated in the passage of the Death Angel that are recorded in the book of Exodus. There was the parting of the water at the Red Sea, the giving of sweet water from the waters of Marah (Exodus 15: 25) and the manna from Heaven when they were in the Wilderness. God rebuked the Israelites for their forgetting of the miracles that He did in Egypt and in the Wilderness because they would not hearken to His voice (Numbers 14: 22). There were some later miracles such as the contest between Elijah and the prophets of Baal on Mount Carmel (I Kings 18: 37 - 38) and the prophet Jonah being swallowed by a whale and delivered safe to the seashore after which he preached to the people of Nineveh. Jesus spoke of this miracle in His discourse and answer to the Pharisees in Matthew 12: 40. Then, the Scriptures record a number of physical miracles during the short three year period of the ministry of Jesus while He was on earth. There was the turning of water to wine in Cana of Galilee (John 2: 11). When He went up to Jerusalem to the Feast of the Passover many believed in His name when they *saw the signs which He did.*" (John 2: 23) Nicodemus came to

Jesus by night to talk with Him on the basis of the miracles that Jesus had performed (John 3: 2). A great multitude followed Him because they saw His miracles (John 6: 2). Jesus rebuked some of the people following the feeding of the multitude because they sought Him, not because they had seen the miracles but because they ate of the loaves and the fish (John 6: 26). Jesus made it clear that He performed physical miracles in order to authenticate His gospel and that people might believe. He gave a summary statement regarding His purpose for miracles before He went to raise Lazarus from the dead. He had received word that Lazarus was sick but He abode in the place where He was ministering for two more days. He announced to His disciples that their friend, Lazarus was sleeping even though He had declared that the sickness was not unto death. Because the disciples did not understand He said to them plainly, *"Lazarus is dead."* (John 11:14) Then He gave a great summary statement for the purpose of His miracles when He said, *"I am glad for your sakes that I was not there, that you **may believe**. Nevertheless let us go to him."* (John 11: 15) Of course, even though Lazarus was raised from the dead, he died again. All of the sick people Jesus healed later died. The son of the widow of Nain was raised up from the dead but he later died. Thus we see that physical miracles were **always temporary**!

Then, there were **Spiritual miracles**. There was His dealing with the demoniac in Capernaum (Luke 4: 31-35). Jesus dealt with a sinful woman at the house of Simon (Luke 7: 36-50). Jesus' dealing with the Gadarene demoniac is another stark illustration of how Jesus changes the life and destiny of men. The people came out and found the demoniac clothed and *"in his **right mind**"* (Mark 5: 1-20). The conversion of Zacchaeus is indelibly imprinted upon the hearts and minds of Christians through the centuries. It was another great spiritual miracle (Luke 19: 1-10). Of course, no discussion of spiritual miracles would be complete without the account of the greatest, most miraculous conversion of the centuries, which was the conversion of the apostle Paul on the road to Damascus (Acts 9: 1-18). This conversion is discussed more fully in other parts of this book but we mention that conversion here in an illustrative manner.

As the Apostolic Age drew to a close, the need for physical miracles to authenticate the Word of God diminished.

New Covenant

As Jesus neared His hour of crucifixion, He addressed His disciples saying, *"With fervent desire I have desired to eat this **Passover** with you before I **suffer**."* (Luke 22: 15) The next day He would become the substitute for the Pascal Lamb and would become the *"once for all"* sacrifice for the redemption of all mankind. As He passed the cup to His disciples after supper He said: *"This cup is the **new covenant** in My **blood,** which is shed for you."* (Luke 22: 20) It was clear that there would be a new covenant that would guide the church that Jesus declared that He would build in Matthew 16:18. The new covenant was confirmed in those last hours before Jesus was arrested when He said, *"When He, the Spirit of truth has come, He will **guide you into all truth;** for he will not speak on His own authority, but whatever He hears Hw will speak; and He will tell you things to come."* (John 16: 13) As the truth of the Gospel was recorded through the inspiration of the Holy Spirit, it became the conveyor of truth to the world with the recording of the miracles of Jesus Himself as the authentication of that truth.

Don't Miss the Truth

Some people miss the great truth and blessing of God because they can only think of miracles in terms of physical miracles that are **always temporary**. Sadly enough, there are some religious charlatans who try to fake those physical miracles. To be sure, there are occasions when we see some physical miracles but they are very rare and they usually serve to strengthen the **faith** and **belief** of Christians. If, however, we miss the great power of spiritual miracles that take place every day as lives are changed for **eternity** with Jesus Christ, we will never understand the place of miracles in the church.

The word that is translated miracles is dunameon (δυναμεων). It is from the root word dunamis that means **power**. Our word dynamite comes from it. Dunameon literally means "**works of power**". The thing we must remember is that it connects **works** and **power**. Sometimes it refers to inherent ability. It is works of such a nature that it **cannot** be produced by **natural means** and has its' **origin in God**. Some scholars believe that the age of miracles ended with the passing of the apostles. Others believe that miracles still happen only at the behest of God and that He does not use human instrumentality as He once did. Both views are lacking. This letter written to the Corinthians in which the gift of miracles is presented was penned by the apostle **Paul**. What was the **greatest miracle** that he ever encountered? It was on the Damascus road when this man who was making "havoc" of the church was struck down and the Lord appeared unto him. There was a great light that blinded him. In that experience, Paul was changed from a vicious persecutor of Christians into one of the greatest advocates for Christ the world has ever known.

Mightiest Works of God

We are not necessarily referring to people here who can part waters or raise the dead. But, those things are not the mightiest works of God. God performs great and mighty works every day of our lives and the greatest miracle that we will ever see is the kind of miracle that Paul experienced when lives, hearts and attitudes are completely reversed. Every Pastor has seen that great miracle of **regeneration** take place before his very eyes. There are men and women who once experienced only the *"works of the flesh ... which are: adultery, fornication, uncleanness, licentiousness, idolatry, sorcery, hatred, contentions, jealousies, outbursts of wrath, selfish ambitions, dissensions, heresies, envy, murders, drunkenness, revelries, and the like."* (Galatians 5: 19-21)   Paul warns that those people will not inherit the Kingdom of God. How many times have we seen that kind of person **regenerated** by the power of the **Holy Spirit of God** and they have entirely different kinds of manifestations in their life. We refer to them as "fruits of the **Spirit**". They are: *"love, joy, peace, longsuffering, kindness, goodness, faithfulness. gentleness, self-control."* (Verses 22 - 23)

This writer once witnessed a man who was vicious and mean according to his own testimony. One night he ran his own 85 year old father out into the woods with nothing but his night shirt on. There were icicles everywhere. It was so cold. He ran two sawmills. The men who worked for him were afraid of him. The Spirit of God directed me to go to him and witness to him. We sat at his kitchen table. All the time I was witnessing he played with a butcher knife. I did not know whether or not he would use the knife on me or if he was just going to continue chopping up match sticks into little bits. Finally, I asked him if he would like to receive Christ as his own Savior that night. He said he did. He **prayed to receive Christ**. He was **immediately changed**. When we got up he asked me if I would like a piece of cake. His wife had made a glazed chocolate cake and he used that butcher knife that he had played with all during the witnessing session to cut a slice of cake instead of cutting me. He became a gentle, tender, humble man who was exactly the opposite of what he had been. Everyone around him knew that they had seen the **miracle** of **salvation** and how it changes the life of any person.

Greatest Miracle Workers

The church with the good fortune of those "**mighty workers**" in the congregation is fortunate indeed. That personal worker who often leads lost people to faith in Jesus Christ, is one of the greatest miracle workers in the world. Of course, the miracle of salvation does not originate with that personal worker but it originates with **God**. We saw it in the life of Zacchaeus when he met Jesus and received **Him** his entire life was changed to the point that he stood and said: *"Lord, I give half of my goods to the poor; and if I have taken anything from anyone by false accusation, I restore fourfold."* Jesus summed up what had happened to Zacchaeus when He said, *"Today salvation has come to this house, because he also is a son of Abraham."* It was at that point that Jesus stated His **greatest purpose** when He said, *"The son of man has come to seek and to save that which was lost."* (Luke 19: 8-10) Yes, Jesus healed some sick people and raised the dead but they all died physically later on. We must **reiterate**, those miracles were **temporary**. Those who **were** and **have been** saved through the centuries having received **eternal life** will **live** with **Him** forever. That is the **greatest miracle** that we will **ever witness.**

This word that is translated "miracle" is not only manifested through **changed lives** but it can also be manifested in **natural victories**. We remember an 85 year old lady who was the last charter member of her church. She was diagnosed with leukemia. The church did not want to give her up. She was a great humble influence. The church went to prayer. The doctors were certain that their diagnosis was correct and we have no doubt that it was but she was later tested and proved to be free of leukemia. This is not to say that it happens in every case but sometimes things happen simply for the **glory of God** and everyone in that small town knew what had happened in the life of the dear lady. Of course, she later passed on but the power of the **Holy Spirit of God** was manifested through her life. Most pastors can attest to similar situations. Yes, God still performs miracles and He uses human instrumentality in the greatest miracle of all - **salvation**!!

Easy to Believe

Because of this it is easy to believe in miracles. Some have described a miracle as an "unmistakable, immediate and powerful action of God." Friend, that is what regeneration, the rebirth is! Others say that miracles "indicate the presence of the Kingdom of God, and authenticate the ministry of Jesus and His church." That too is true! Every time a soul is saved heaven rejoices. Every time a person is saved, the ministry, mission, death burial and resurrection of Jesus Christ is authenticated. Salvation is the **miracle of miracles!!**

As stated previously, like Healing, there are two types of miracles: physical miracles and spiritual miracles. Physical miracles are merely temporal but a spiritual miracle is always eternal. Salvation is **forever!!**

So, the question is still being asked by many: "Does God still do miracles today?" Yes, of course, **GOD** does! But, only **GOD** does!

The Two Types

Every pastor has observed both kinds of miracles. This author has observed many spiritual miracles. One particular one comes to mind. One pastor relates this story. While a visiting evangelist was on the church field leading in an evangelistic effort the evangelist declared that he wanted to visit the roughest man in the small town. The pastor thought and decided to take the evangelist to the man who lived next door to the church. The man had just been freed from prison for murdering his wife. He was a secluded individual who did not relate well to other people but the pastor decided to take the evangelist there to visit. The visit started out to be a normal visit and then the evangelist began to share the Gospel. The felon began to weep profusely. When the evangelist asked him if he would like to give his heart to the Lord the man fell on his knees and began to pray about all the sins of his past. He repented and trusted Christ as his savior and later joined the church and was baptized. That, dear reader, is a miracle! Who performed that great miracle? God did of course!

Physical Miracles

It should be noted that physical miracles are not the norm but spiritual miracles are! Those Christians who have the gift of miracles should be enlisted to lead the outreach and soul winning ministries of the Church.

They should also be enlisted to lead ministries to the special needs of people as well as the sick and needy because they are usually always very compassionate and caring people.

Prophecy: The word for this gift is propheteia (προφητεία). This simply refers to "one who speaks forth." A prophet is not simply a glorified fortune teller but a proclaimer of divine messages. It also means "one in whom the message of God springs forth." It is **speaking forth divine counsel**. That person who has the ability to preach or teach the Word of God is working in a prophetic role. It carries the connotation of **boldness**. There were times in the Old Testament when prophets warned the people of things to come. Thank God, we still have prophets among us today! That faithful pastor who stands in the pulpit to "tell forth" the Word of God is prophesying. That pastor who warns of the consequences of sin and debauchery and where it will lead our country is prophesying. That Sunday School teacher who faithfully declares the word of God to a class on Sunday is prophesying. That youth worker who is faithfully teaching the principles from God's Word to the youth is prophesying. Thank God for the gift of prophecy. It is another gift that cannot be "ginned up" or "developed" apart from the **Holy Spirit** of God!

The Pastor/Prophet

The pastor functions in the role of the prophet in the local church. He is a spokesperson for God to His people in that church. He admonishes, warns, encourages, teaches and counsels with God's people in the local church. The Spirit powered church must have a pastor/prophet leading if it is to be successful.

In the Old Testament one of the most important roles of the prophet was to pray. He was to pray for the mind of the Lord. He was to pray to receive a clear understanding of what God was doing in and thru and for His people. So must the pastor of a Spirit powered church be a prayer warrior who spends much time before Holy God on behalf of his people and the church. Leonard Ravenhill in his book, *Why Revival Tarries,* says, "Men of prayer must be men of steel, for they will be assaulted by Satan even before they attempt to assault Satan's Kingdom. He must pray for the people of his congregation because he cares for their souls. Wealthy is the church that has a "praying prophet" in their pulpit Sunday by Sunday, for He is the **Shepherd** of **their souls**!!.

Also in the Old Testament the prophet watched over the Word of the Lord. He handled the word with humility, honor and boldness. He shouted out the word of the Lord to the people. (They did not have sound systems in those days.) Our day calls for such men to stand in the pulpit and boldly proclaim, "*thus says the Lord.*" A Spirit powered church will be declaring the Word of the Lord to a lost generation and the pastor/prophet will be leading the way. In a day of compromising, mediocre, ear tickling preaching we desperately need men who will stand strong and preach a prophetic word from God to His people. The pastor/prophet will be like a trumpet with a certain sound telling the truth in a land of deceitfulness!! He will proclaim the word even if it is not "politically correct" to do so.

The Watchman

God gave the word to Ezekiel, the prophet of the exile. Before his captivity, he was a young man and was familiar with the prophet Jeremiah, the weeping prophet, who prophesied Israel's captivity. He understood well what happens when the voice of the Prophet is muffled and the nation finds itself without a prophetic voice. It was in chapter 3 of his prophecy that Ezekiel nailed it when he described the responsibility of the prophet. Here is what God said: "***Son of man, I have made you a watchman for the house of Israel; therefore hear a word from My mouth, and give them warning from Me: when I say to the wicked, 'You shall surely die,' and you give him no warning, nor speak to warn the wicked from his wicked way, to save his life, that same wicked man shall die in his iniquity; but his blood I will require at your hand. Yet, if you warn the wicked, and he does not turn from his wickedness, nor from his wicked way, he shall die in his iniquity; but you have delivered your soul.*"** (Ezekiel 3:17-19) There stands one of the great prophesies of the Old Testament like a great lighthouse guiding the pastor/prophet away from the dangerous, rocky shoals of compromise, mediocrity, intimidation, job security or "*itching ears.*" (II Timothy 4: 3) The charge to "*watch*" did not end with Ezekiel. It was among Paul's final instructions to Timothy. After warning Timothy of a time when men would not endure sound doctrine Paul said, "*But you be **watchful** in all things, endure afflictions, do the work of an evangelist, fulfill your ministry.*" (II Timothy 4: 5). **It does not get any clearer than that!**

The prophet in the Old Testament was also a watchman. He cared for the souls of the people. He took it as a personal responsibility to care for and watch over the flock of God. He also was a watchman that sounded the alarm to God's people when situations in the land turned ungodly. People are often naïve and need someone to give them spiritual guidance. At the same time, people of our generation are biblically illiterate and they need someone who will stand strong on biblical morals and ethics, not compromising with a tainted world view. The Spirit powered church must be lead by a man who will stand in the gap and proclaim the truth about our world even when men do not want to hear it and may even be willing to harm the prophet for declaring the truth of God!

The most important task of the pastor/prophet of this day is to seek and know the will of God for the church he serves. The most important aspect of the pastor/prophet's responsibility is that of being a visionary. So many churches are floundering and losing their way because they did not have the right direction in the beginning. If the man of God has no vision for the church, is it logical for us to expect the congregation to have a vision for the direction of the church? I think not! The man of God must seek the face of **God** and get **His** direction for the church. Then he must lead the church to be visionary; so as to accomplish the will and plan of God. The Spirit powered church will be a church where the **Word** is being proclaimed no matter the consequences. It is a place where the truth is told, whatever may come. The world is being watched by the prophet no matter how intimidating it seems. Those who hold the responsibility for teaching and proclaiming the **Word of God** most certainly should possess this special and wonderful gift of **prophecy.** All of this must be done by those who are "moved with compassion!"

Discernment: Another of the spiritual gifts is that of "discerning of spirits". This word is translated from the Greek word diakriseis (διακρίσεις). The word means "to separate out" or "to learn by discriminating". The same root word is used in Matthew 16:3 when Jesus talks about discerning weather conditions by the sky. It also means to test, prove or scrutinize so as to decide. It has to do with judging by evidence whether something is good or evil. A discerning Christian will not accept the words or deeds of a person who feigns Christianity unless he sees some fruits of the Spirit that are clearly marked out in Galatians 5 where Paul makes it clear that the "*works of the flesh*" and "*fruits of the Spirit*" cannot be comingled!!. This kind of person has insight. He does not always accept surface claims unless there is some real evidence to support them. He can spot false prophets and false teachers a mile away. Every church needs some mature Christians with discernment. John warned about such people in I John 4: 1 where he said: *"Beloved, do not believe every spirit, but **test** the spirits, whether they are of God; because many false prophets have gone out into the world."*

Discerning of Spirits

It is well to remember that this gift is about the *"**discerning of spirits**"*. It is not something that can be done by a palmist who is supposedly "reading the lines" in your hand. It is not the shrewdness of a poker player nor is it the insightfulness of a personnel director. There is a **spiritual** dimension to this gift. It is marked out in I Corinthians 2: 14 which says: *"... the **natural** man does not receive the things of the Spirit of God, for they are foolishness to him; nor can he know them, because they are **spiritually discerned**."* Until one responds to the prompting of the Holy Spirit and knows Jesus Christ as Savior, he cannot possibly have the mind of Christ (verse 16). Until one has the "mind of Christ" the things of God will be "**foolishness**" to him. It is for this reason that the world often sees Christians as a bit odd. Sometimes, the people of the world will even conclude that devoted Christians have mental problems. They never understand the work of the **Holy Spirit** in the Christian's life. This gift of **discernment** may also be possessed in conjunction with other spiritual gifts such as wisdom, faith or knowledge.

What Happens Without It

What happens in a Church where there are no leaders who possess this gift of **discernment of Spirits**? We have a graphic example of it in the church at Corinth to which Paul was writing this letter.

The church at Corinth was abusing the Lord's Supper (I Corinthians 11: 17-34). There were divisions in the church (Verses 17-18). There were heresies among them (verse 19). When they came together it was not that they might observe the Lord's supper but it was for the purpose of "showing off" before others. In eating, everyone was taking his supper to eat before others. Some were hungry and others were drunken. There was no spirit of sharing. Paul declared to them that whoever would eat the bread and drink the cup of the Lord unworthily, would be guilty of the body and blood of the Lord. He charged them to examine themselves before they did eat the bread and drink the cup. He emphasized the consequences of their sin by warning them that they were eating and drinking judgment to themselves *"not **discerning** the Lord's **body**"* (Verse 29). Paul pointed out the terrible price they were paying for their sin when he said, "... *for this reason many are **weak** and **sick** among you, and many **sleep**"* and why are they drinking "*judgment*" unto themselves? It was because they were partaking of the Lord's supper in an unworthy manner. It was a desecration of the **ordinance** of God as well as the **house** of God. The grave problem was that they did so "*not **discerning the Lord's body.**"* (Verse 29) Because the judgment of God had come upon them, some were weak, others were sick, and some had died. **Those who abuse the Lord's body will always pay a terrible price for their sin**. This passage teaches us clearly that a Christian can send himself to an early grave by besmirching things holy and bringing reproach to the Lord's body, the **Church**. It is after Paul rebukes the church for their conduct that he begins, in the next chapter, to talk about the gifts of the Spirit.

The Blessed Church

Blessed is the church with a goodly number of members with spiritual discernment. They will keep the church from a lot of heartache and grief. It is safe to say that most pastors have known of those who would come into the church for "business" reasons or for prestige. There are those charlatans who will come into a church and seek to gain authority and a following or demand authority in the church on the hint that they will give money. More than one church has compromised their convictions trying to "hold on" to a person like that when it would have been much better to let them leave than to break up the fellowship of the church. Of course, the best solution is that such people would repent and gain a right relationship with God. The people who were desecrating the Lord's Supper were doing so because they did not understand what the Body of Christ was all about. That is a sad commentary on the life of any church.

Remember the Dangers of Satan

We must remember that Satan desires to destroy the church. He will use any means available to him. That means that he often slips into the church in some of the most unexpected ways. That is where spiritual discernment becomes so important to the local church. Let's recap. Spiritual discernment, plain and simple, is the ability to understand and make application of the Word of God with an emphasis on deciding what is true and what is false. All Christians could have the **gift of discernment** if they would spend time with God. James 1:5 tells us that anyone can ask God for wisdom and it will be given. If the Christian has no discernment he will fall for anything. A lack of discernment in the life of a Christian is a real sign of spiritual immaturity.

The Present Condition

In these trying times the gift of discernment is essential in order to have a Spirit powered church. The world has **infiltrated** the very heart of the church. Those who are of this world have ideas of their own as to how a church should be led and operated. Many times these imposters destroy any spiritual ray of hope the church might possess.

The gift of discernment enables the believer to determine whether an action, deed, word or motive is of God or of Satan. Spiritual discernment involves a keen spiritual insight that can only be possessed by one who has spent much time in the presence of the Lord. The gift of discernment is used as an agent of **protection** to the congregation. Discernment is a gift that protects the church against the "the wiles of the devil". In the same way, a discerning heart can determine what is of the **Holy Spirit** and what is not. Many are doing hurtful things in the church while contending that the Holy Spirit prompted them to do it. While the Holy Spirit does lead Christians to do specific things, He will never prompt us to do anything that does not **coincide with Scripture.**

Example

In one particular church, there was a movement in the congregation to ask for the pastor's resignation. Emotions were running high in a business meeting in the church when a woman stood and loudly proclaimed that the pastor was not "her pastor" and that the Holy Spirit was prompting her to ask him to resign. Of course, anyone who has a close walk with **God** knows that **He** is not the author of confusion and the **Holy Spirit** would never prompt someone to do something like that in public. The Holy Spirit is not in the business of publicly embarrassing and ridiculing the man of **God!**

In a day when truth is constantly at war with error the church **must** be able to discern what is of God and what is not. The church **must** separate truth from error! The Christian who desires discernment **must** spend much time in the word. Knowledge of the Bible will also create in us the ability to discern right from wrong.

An Enabler

Spiritual discernment enables the **Christian** and the **church** to know the will of God in every situation. This gift is especially useful when the church has big decisions to make. It enables the believer to invite and allow the Holy Spirit to work in the church and the individual life. Henry Blackaby in his book ***Experiencing God*** says the "Christian should find where God is working and then join Him." This is where the gift of discernment fits. The Spirit powered church needs to always be discerning as to where God is at work and what God wants them to do. Then that church should get actively involved in the ministry.

Spiritual discernment will always help the Christian to make the kind of choices that will bring spiritual maturity and become good stewards of what God has given them. It will help the Christian develop biblical values, ethics and morals and ultimately a proper Christian world view. Spiritual warfare is real in the Christian life and spiritual discernment enables the Christian to "fight the good fight" and be victorious over Satan.

The Christian who is gifted with discernment can readily spot worldliness and worldly ideals. The church needs to be able to distinguish between **real holiness** and a "**form of Godliness**."

Enlisting of Workers

Finally, it is especially important that members of the nominating committee, in its' task of enlisting workers for church positions, be gifted in the area of discernment. Wise choices of leaders and workers will insure the future well being of the Church and its work. Haphazard choosing of leaders will always cause harm to the church and sometimes destroy the unity as well. It is a simple concept. The Spirit powered church needs spiritually discerning Christians as members in order to do the work of God successfully. Whether the discernment is used in the members' personal lives, the corporate worship of the church or to help someone else in his or her spiritual journey, it is a most valuable gift that God has given to the church.

Tongues: Another Spiritual gift was that of "*different kinds of tongues.*" (I Corinthians 12: 10) We have discussed the matter of tongues earlier but suffice it to say that there were apparently some in the church at Corinth who were trying to imitate Pentecost. Paul is seeking to impart to the Corinthian church a proper understanding of "tongues". We must forever remember that the proper understanding of tongues on the day of Pentecost and in other references in the New Testament were references to **language**. We must never forget that the people on the day of Pentecost said, "...*how is it that we hear, each in our* **own language** *in which we were* **born?**" The Holy Spirit used this method of spreading the gospel on several occasions. In Corinth, however, where the church had divisions, and had desecrated a sacred thing like the **Lord's Supper**; there was also misunderstanding about the gift of tongues.

In the following chapter, Paul points out that without love, these gifts are nothing. In fact, he suggests that without love they are **hypocritical**. They may be copied but not possessed unless one is filled with love as well as the Holy Spirit of God. He points out a time when some of these gifts will no longer be needed and that "*where there are* **tongues, they shall cease.**" (I Corinthians 13: 8) Many scholars believe that tongues ceased when the New Testament was completed and people had the word of God in its' fullness to guide them in their Christian lives. It is the belief of this writer that these spiritual skills still exist but, sometimes, in a **different form**. For instance, I met a young school teacher in Virginia who teaches in the public schools there. She teaches foreign languages. She told me that she had a gift for languages. She was interested in studying Greek. I sent her an old seminary textbook that I used several years ago in Beginner's Greek. It would be almost impossible for one to go to the mission field without the gift of language. Moreover, there is the gift of **interpretation**. There have been numerous times when great men such as Billy Graham have preached the gospel in foreign countries through an interpreter. This is a special gift that many people have. I have always known that evangelists who preach through an interpreter always desire that the interpreter be a Christian who is **filled** with the **Spirit**. Every Christian and every church will do well to heed the plea of the great apostle Paul when he said: "... **earnestly** *desire the best gifts.*" (I Corinthians 12: 31) He closes out the chapter pointing out to them a more excellent way that he sets out in chapter 13 which we often refer to as the chapter of love.

The great apostle spends chapter 14 instructing the Corinthians concerning the matter of tongues and cautions them against phoniness. Apparently, there were some in the church who had begun to use ecstatic utterances in the service to "edify" or build up themselves. Paul reminded them that they might be building up themselves but it was not **edifying** to the **church**. He points out to them that it is much better to prophesy (tell forth the gospel) than to speak in a tongue that no one understands (verses 4-5). Of this matter Paul says: "*... I would rather speak five words with my understanding, that I might teach others also, than ten thousand words in a tongue.*" (verse 19) Paul clearly indicates that the best gifts are those that **clearly communicate** the gospel in a manner that can be understood. As pointed out earlier, one Christian may possess more than one of these gifts but happy is the church that is made up of Spirit filled people who possess these spiritual gifts. They are essential to a church with the desire for a victorious ministry.

There are some churches that have taken this gift to extreme ends. The misuse of tongues has brought division and destruction to some churches. Many Bible believing churches have split as a result of the misuse of this gift. God is not the author of confusion. He expects all things in the church to be done **decently** and in **order**. The gift of tongues was never meant to bring attention to the **person speaking** but to bring attention to the **gospel of Jesus Christ**.

Our Time

The way tongues can be described in churches of our day is the wonderful ability of people to speak different languages fluently in order for the gospel to be spread. That was what happened at Pentecost. Tongues at Pentecost were not unknown, ecstatic utterance or "heavenly" language; it was a manifestation of God's power in that **everyone present** heard the gospel in his **own language**.

With an influx of many from other countries entering the United States there is the need for these people to hear the "good news" in their own native tongue. We must cultivate the gift of tongues (languages) so many will come to Christ. A friend of this writer has the gift of tongues. He is a missionary to Romania. He does not speak in an unknown or "ecstatic language", but he does posses the ability to **learn languages** quickly and efficiently. God has gifted him to do mission work in other countries by gifting him with the ability to comprehend and master other languages. He has served on the mission field in Mexico, Romania and China. He speaks Spanish, Romanian and a dialect of Chinese. Because of this gift he has been instrumental in planting churches and winning the lost to Jesus in several parts of the world. A Spirit powered church will use such a gift to reach the different cultures around it by allowing those with the gift of languages to serve and share their faith. Some churches have language groups meeting in their church building.

One final thought about glossalalia; which means more to the Kingdom of God, a person who can speak in an "unknown" tongue that no one understands or a person who is gifted to speak other languages? The answer is simple: it is more important to win the lost than to speak in an unknown tongue!

Conclusion

The apostle Paul is careful to emphasize that each spiritual gift is to be recognized in the body of the church for its' value and not for the self aggrandizement of individuals. These gifts are for the edifying of the **body** of Christ , which is the church. If one gift only is exalted, it tends to make the church into some kind of freakish organism. He says, for instance: *"the body is not one member but many"* (I Corinthians 12: 14) He continues by stating that the foot is not to say *"because I am not a hand I am not of the body."* The ear is not to say *"because I am not an eye I am not of the body."* Then he gives the punch line: *"If the whole body were an eye, where would be the hearing? If the whole were hearing, where would be the smelling?"* He points out that God has created the body in such a way that even the less comely parts are **important** and **necessary** to the proper functioning of the **entire body**. A body with only an eye would be a monster and Paul is suggesting that if a church emphasizes only one gift (which was happening at Corinth) it would be a freakish church that would not be effective. The Corinthian church had gone overboard on the matter of speaking in tongues, which, was not the same thing that happened at Pentecost. It had caused confusion. Paul compared it to a trumpet with an uncertain sound (I Corinthians 14: 8-9). He warned them that unless they uttered words that can be understood, no one would understand what was spoken. He warned that if the unlearned or unbelievers came into the church they could not receive any message from what was said. His question was, *"Will they not say that you are out of your mind?"* (I Corinthians 14: 23) Paul is saying that there must be spiritual balance in the church. The real purpose of spiritual gifts is to edify (or build up) the **church** When the diverse members work for the same purpose they complement one another and it becomes a church with a message for a lost world. The pastor is the overseer. He is the shepherd. He is a minister but he is joined in the ministry by other Christians who are Spirit **filled** and committed. Those **teachers** are important. The **nursery wor**kers are important. The **ushers** are important. The **musicians** are important. The **custodians** are important. When these positions are all occupied by Spirit filled people, the church will be great in the work of the **kingdom of God** regardless of its' size. The Spirit powered church will have mastered the art of harnessing the Gifts of the Spirit when it stops being **afraid** of the Holy Spirit and begin to allow **Him** and **His gifts** to empower **His church**.

Five Steps

The church that will follow the **five steps** set out in this book will be a church with a **victorious ministry** wherever that church may be located. It will not happen overnight nor in one outstanding revival although great revivals have been a catalyst to the development of great Sprit filled churches. It will not happen without some satanic opposition but if a church will follow the biblical principles set forth here year after year and never compromise these principles, that church will develop a great Christ honoring ministry. In this chapter we have emphasized the gifts as listed in I Corinthians 12 because they are presented as being so essential to the unity of the body of Christ. As pointed out, there is also a listing of gifts in Ephesians 4: 11 where they are pointing to the unity of the faith. Another listing appears in Romans 12: 6 - 8. These listings are not identical but they teach us that the Holy Spirit of God bestows upon the members of Christ's body, the church, those gifts that are needful for the unity of the church and the propagation of the gospel in every culture and in every age. These scriptures suggest that the listing of **spiritual gifts** were not **closed** at the end of the New Testament. For instance, there are Christians in the church today who possess the gift of **technology**. They can understand computers and projection screens. They can build a sound system so that the gospel can be properly heard. There are those who have **diverse musical skills** who contribute much to the worship of God in the body of Christ. There are those who have **secretarial gifts** that are so essential in helping the church to stay in touch with the members of the body. There are those who have **medical skills** who are invaluable in assisting the church to care for the health of the needy. There are those who have **maintenance skills** who are so essential in keeping the church building clean and beautiful as well as comfortable. There are those who have **driving skills** who are necessary in assisting the church in accomplishing their mission in the world such as disaster relief. There are those who have **interpersonal skills** that are so helpful in greeting people and making them comfortable as they visit the church. All of these gifts originate from the **Holy Spirit** who is active in every facet of our lives. In Exodus 31: 3-5 we have the record of God speaking to Moses and informing him that He has filled Bezaleel with the Spirit of God including wisdom and understanding and the knowledge of all manner of **workmanship** and all of his skills were a gift of the Spirit. This tells us how **unlimited** the Spirit of God is and it also tells us that the working of the Holy Spirit in our lives is **unlimited**. It is our prayer that the readers of this book will grasp that **marvelous unrestricted power** of the **Holy Spirit of God** in their lives and in their churches, all to the eternal glory of the **Triune God.**

POINTS FOR DISCUSSION

1. Dr. Elmer Towns gives an excellent definition of a spiritual gift. He says: "A spiritual gift is spiritual in character, sovereignly given by God the Holy Spirit, to minister to others, in the power of God, with an evident manifestation of the Holy Spirit through the Christian as he serves God." Do you agree with Dr. Towns? Why or why not?

2. There are diversities of gifts, differences of administration, and diversity of operations bestowed by the triune God and that spiritual gifts are given **not to exalt one individual** but to profit **everyone**. They are for the common good in the life of the church. Explain why the Spiritual gifts have been given for the good of the whole church.

3. It is sometimes very easy for Christians to conclude, erroneously, that wisdom is a sign of human intelligence. One writer says, *"... on the contrary true wisdom really is a moral quality."* Churches must always remember that worldly wisdom or human wisdom is not equated with **Godly wisdom**. Please explain the difference between worldly wisdom and Godly wisdom.

4. True wisdom always begins with living under the rule and power of the triune God. The scriptures have a word on the subject: *"the fear of the Lord is the beginning of wisdom: A good understanding have all those who do His commandments."* (Psalms 111: 10 NKJV) Discuss the content of this verse seeking to understand the truth about Godly wisdom.

5. A church cannot function properly from the wisdom of man or the wisdom of the world. Worldly wisdom originates in the human heart that is not in tune with God. This is the kind of wisdom that is associated with the idea of *"doing"* church like a business. The church cannot be operated like a secular business by secular rules of economics. What happens in the church when we try to use worldly wisdom to guide it? Give some examples.

6. Do you agree with the authors when they say "people of wisdom should always be assigned to the decision making committees of the church because that is where churches most

often go astray. For instance, the pastor search committee should always be occupied by men and women of wisdom." Why or why not?

Epilogue

To those Christians across this nation who feel enshrouded by **discouragement** and **despondency** we simply **must** say that the Holy Spirit of God does not always act in dramatic fashion. It is not always a matter of glitz, flashing lights or blaring speakers. To be sure, there are occasions reported in the Scripture when the Holy Spirit has worked in dramatic fashion such as: creation, the deliverance of the children of Israel from captivity, Elijah's Mount Carmel experience and the experience of Pentecost. There are examples in history of special outpourings of the Holy Spirit such as: the first and second Great Awakenings, the Protestant Reformation, the Hebrides revival and the revival of 1858. These, however, were rare occurrences over many centuries. This does not mean that the Holy Spirit is not at work every single hour of every single day of our lives. It is to say that the Spirit usually works in a quiet way which is what Elijah had to learn after the Mount Carmel experience (I Kings 18: 20-46).

After Jezebel threatened his life, Elijah fled to the wilderness below Beersheba where he finally sat under a Juniper tree overwhelmed with discouragement and despair. An angel of the Lord came and fed him there. The angel then returned a second time when he touched him and said, "... *the journey is too great for you.*" (I Kings 19:7) **What a lesson for every Christian!** The journeys of life are too much for us without the power and help of the Holy Spirit of God. Never forget that there are always those Jezebels around who are willing to threaten, intimidate or otherwise harass the faithful Christian.

Elijah, engulfed by a spirit of fear and discouragement, went down to Mount Horeb which is known as the "Mount of God". There he entered into a cave as though to hibernate. Fear and discouragement are always debilitating to the Christian life. What a terrible scene for the great man of God who had been so empowered by the Spirit of God and had been mightily used of God to accomplish such great things. No wonder the Lord addressed him with that disturbingly pungent and pertinent question: "*What are you doing here, Elijah?*" (I Kings 19:9) That was certainly no place or condition for the servant of God. Elijah was discouraged because

143

of the condition of Israel and he wanted to die. The Lord sent a strong and mighty wind to the mountain. It was so fierce that it broke the rocks to pieces but the Lord's voice was not in the wind. After that he sent an earthquake but the Lord was not in the earthquake. After the earthquake came fire but the Lord was not in the fire. After the fire came a **still small voice** and Elijah was more shaken by that still small voice than of the great events that he had witnessed. He wrapped his face in his mantle and went to the entrance of the cave. The Lord spoke to him in that still small voice and insisted that he face the question again: "*What are you doing here, Elijah?*" (I Kings 19: 13) Elijah started his spiel again about the terrible conditions in Israel and, as usually happens with a discouraged and fearful person, he exaggerated the situation. That is frighteningly easy for any Christian to do. While Elijah was convinced that everyone in Israel had turned away from God, he had to be reminded that there were 7,000 in Israel who had not bowed the knee to Baal (I Kings 19: 18).

God then commanded Elijah to anoint Hazael and Jehu as well as Elisha who would take Elijah's place. Elisha was plowing when he was called. Elijah may have wondered why God would select a plowboy to follow him after his faithfulness and the great deeds that God had performed through him. It must have been humbling for Elijah to learn that it doesn't take much to follow the one who runs in fear or discouragement and that **God always makes the difference**. It is **God** who takes a very ordinary but **obedient** person and makes him **great**..

Pastor, Christian Worker, the same God who came to Elijah in his moment of desperation is still alive and He is **totally available** to you. Our God, through His Holy Spirit, is still at work in the world and in our lives even when things seem so desperate. It may be that time when the Holy Spirit has intervened with strong conviction in the heart and life of that lost person to whom you were witnessing. It may be the Holy Spirit's direction in your life or ministry. It may have been the Spirit's encouragement when things seemed so hopeless in your life or your Christian work. It may have been the Spirit providing for you as you studied and prepared for your life's calling. It may have been the Spirit's work and power in opening doors of service for you or he may have prevented you from making some terrible mistake in your life or ministry. It may have been the Spirit's guidance to the correct physician who found the development of cells in your body in the early stages that would have taken your life and yet you were spared. It may have been the Lord's providing for your financial and physical needs in unexpected and mysterious ways.

The intervention of the **Spirit** in evangelism is illustrated in the conversion of a very successful merchant that I knew several years ago. He was very personable and had friends everywhere. He was morally upright. He did not use beverage alcohol but he had never accepted Jesus Christ as his savior. I had presented the gospel to him. He had been to church numerous times and had heard the gospel presented repeatedly. As I was to learn later, there were some things in his life that he did not want to give up even though he was morally upright and a good provider for his family. Late one evening he sent for me. He had been checking stock in preparation to order more merchandise. He had been concerned about his soul for days but on that evening he began to weep profusely about his soul and his lost condition. He had experienced that "now or never" conviction that often accompanies conversion. That night he accepted Christ as his savior. The next morning, in a snow storm, he made his way to church and made an open and public confession of Jesus Christ as his savior. I was privileged to baptize him and from that time forward he became a very faithful and humble servant of his Lord and his church. He never looked back! He no longer desired a form of recreation that he was so hesitant to give up. It was a perfect example of the quiet and even mysterious way that the Holy Spirit often works in our lives. William Cowper, the great hymn writer, said it well:

"God moves in a mysterious way
His wonders to perform;
He plants his footsteps in the sea
And rides upon the storm.

Deep in unfathomable mines
Of never failing skill
He treasures up His bright designs
And works His sovereign will.

Ye fearful saints, fresh courage take;
The clouds you so much dread
Are big with mercy and shall break
In blessings on your head.

Judge not the Lord by feeble sense,
But trust Him for His grace;

Behind a frowning providence
He hides a smiling face.

His purpose will ripen fast,
Unfolding every hour;
The bud may have a bitter taste,
But sweet will be the flower.

Thine unbelief is sure to err
And scan His work in vain;
God is His own interpreter,
And He will make it plain."

These lines grew out of Cowper's life when he was in a severe depression. He had called a cabbie and asked that he take him to the Thames river where he intended to commit suicide by drowning. A thick London fog descended and the cabbie lost his way (intentionally or by accident). After aimlessly driving about for awhile, the cabbie let Cowper descend from the cab. Strangely, Cowper was at his own front door. Looking back on that incident Cowper felt that it was God's providential design that kept him from drowning himself. This incident inspired the poem above.

It is our prayer and our hope, dear reader, that you will be alert to the working of the Holy Spirit in the answer to your prayers and that you will earnestly savor those times in your life when the Holy Spirit, in his own quiet way, empowers you and ministers to your every need. We must emphasize it again; everything that was available to Elijah is also available to us. This book goes out with a prayer that every Christian who reads these lines will experience the surging, exhilarating and satisfying power of the **Holy Spirit** that attends the life of every Christian who is in absolute **obedience** to the prompting of the Spirit. We learn from Elijah that things are never as bad as they seem to the discouraged or despondent Christian and that the **Holy Spirit** is always there to attend our ways as we obey His leading. When that is happening, prayer life becomes a refreshingly satisfying joy in the life of any believer.

About the Authors

Robert M. Tenery:

He graduated from Pfeiffer University with a BA Degree and from Southwestern Baptist Theological Seminary with a MDiv. He pastored Baptist Churches for 40 years and is now retired. At the end of his active ministry he served seven and a half years as a Chaplain for the State of North Carolina in which he dealt with the most serious Juvenile Offenders in the State including those who had committed First Degree Murder, First Degree Rape, Armed Robbery, Car Jackings, Arson, Grand Larceny and other crimes. During the last six months he served he saw 61 of those young men become Christians and several are now in the ministry. He also edited **The Southern Baptist Advocate** which went to 64,000 Southern Baptist Pastors and Lay Leaders during the Conservative Resurgence in the Southern Baptist Convention. He has done Ghost Writing for several individuals and has penned some poetry. He served as a Trustee of the Baptist Sunday School Board (Lifeway Christian Resources) for 16 years during which time the Trustees turned the Board back to its' historical roots, brought major improvements to the Sunday School Literature, purchased the Holman Bible Company and revamped the Bookstore System. It was also during his tenure there that the name of the Board was changed to Lifeway Christian Resources although he was never convinced that a change in jargon would solve all the problems. He was privileged to attend meetings of the North American Mission Board where his wife served as a Trustee for eight years and enjoyed the exchange of ideas with other Pastors and Lay Leaders from across the Country. He also served as Vice-President of the Southern Baptist Pastors Conference and President of the North Carolina Baptist Pastors Conference. He served on the Committee on Boards for the SBC, the Church Growth Commission for the North Carolina Convention and the Governor's Commission on Infant Mortality as well as the Juvenile Crime Commission. During his last pastorate, he served on the County's Social Services Board and was Chairman when his tenure ended.

J. Steve Sells:

He graduated from Gardner-Webb University with a BA Degree and Southeastern Baptist Theological Seminary with a MDiv. He served as a Pastor for 35 years before becoming the Director of Missions for Savannah Baptist Association in Savannah, Georgia. He recently became the Director of Missions for the historic Randolph Baptist Association in North Carolina where the Sandy Creek Movement began in 1755. He prepared the Area-wide Preparation Guide for the True Love Waits Program that was launched by the Sunday School Board of the Southern Baptist Convention and has developed special ministries in helping declining and plateaued Churches with Restart and Refocus Programs. He wrote a weekly religious column for 3 years. He is a member of the Society for Church Consulting and a certified Church Health Consultant. He has always emphasized the need of the Holy Spirit in the life of the Church. Denominational Offices he has held include serving as a Trustee of the New Orleans Baptist Theological Seminary for ten years and on the Committee on Nominations for the SBC. He served as Secretary/Treasurer of the North Carolina Baptist Pastors' Conference as well as Vice President of the Conference.